GUITARLELE
BLUES MASTERY FOR BEGINNERS

UKELIKETHEPROS
© 2021 TERRY CARTER

ISBN-13: **9-781735-969237**
UKELIKETHEPROS.COM
© 2021 TERRY CARTER

TABLE OF CONTENTS

GUITARLELE BLUES MASTERY - INTRO	01
HISTORY OF THE BLUES	03
01 - **BLUES FORM**	04
02 - **STRAIGHT VS SWING - 1/8th NOTES**	05
03 - **HOW TO HOLD A PICK**	06
04 - **STRUMMING BLUES IN A**	07
05 - **STRUMMING BLUES IN A -** WITH QUICK CHANGE	08
06 - **STRUMMING BLUES IN A -** WITH MUTES	09
07 - **WALKING THE BLUES IN A**	10
08 - **BOOGIE WOOGIE IN A -** OPEN CHORDS	11
09 - **BOOGIE WOOGIE IN A -** POWER CHORDS	12
10 - **BOOGIE WOOGIE IN B -** CLOSED POWER CHORDS	13
11 - **FINGERSTYLE BLUES IN A**	14
12 - **BLUES ROCK IN A**	15
13 - **BLUES ROCK IN B**	16
14 - **JUMP BLUES IN A**	17
15 - **COUNTRY BLUES IN A**	19
16 - **SLOW 12/8 BLUES IN A**	21
17 - **BLUES SCALE IN A**	23
18 - **BLUES SOLO IN A**	24
TERRY CARTER's MESSAGE FOR YOU	27
THE ESSENTIALS	A
HOW TO READ TAB	B
GUITARLELE PARTS	C
GUITARLELE HANDS	D
NOTES ON THE GUITARLELE NECK	E
UNDERSANDING CHORD DIAGRAMS	F
MUSIC SYMBOLS TO KNOW	G
CHORD CHART	I
BASIC RHYTHMS	K
ESSENTIAL RHYTHMS	L
ABOUT THE AUTHOR	M
ONLINE COURSES	N
TERRY CARTER MUSIC STORE	O

GUITARLELE
BLUES MASTERY FOR BEGINNERS

Welcome to the Guitarlele Blues Mastery book by Uke Like The Pros and written by Terry Carter. This book is the most comprehensive book written for Blues on the Guitarlele in the world. In the Guitarlele Blues Mastery book you are going to learn how to play all styles of Blues rhythm, fingerstyle, and picking on this wonderful six-string instrument called the guitarlele.

In this book you are going to explore all the techniques and tools that you need to become a Guitarlele Blues Master. You are going to learn Blues Shuffle, Walking Blues, Blues Rock, Fingerstyle Blues, Boogie Woogie Blues, Jump Blues, Country Blues, Slow Blues, Jazz Blues, Blues Scales, and Blues Soloing.

Before we jump into the contents of the Guitarlele Blues Mastery book, let's break down the guitarlele. The guitarlele, also known as the guilele or guitalele, is a 6-string ukulele that is tuned (from low to high) A-D-G-C-E-A. Strings 1-4 (G-C-E-A) are the same as a ukulele, but the guitarlele adds the low D and A strings. Guitarleles typically come in two sizes, the tenor (17-inch scale length) and the baritone (20-inch scale length). Scale length is the measurement from the inside of the nut to the inside of the saddle. Some of the top guitarleles are made by KoAloha, Kanilea, Romero Creations, Kala, and Ohana.

Although you could play everything in this book on the guitar (E-A-D-G-B-E), the tuning would not match the audio backing tracks that are included with this book. Nor would the tuning match the complete video course of all these lessons that is sold separately at ukelikethepros.com/guitareleblues

The Uke Like The Pros Guitarlele Blues Mastery book is a step-by-step introduction to the Blues, which means each lesson will build upon the next, so that you develop the proper techniques and confidence you need to become a Blues Master.

One of the key concepts in this book is understanding the difference between Swing and Straight Feel. This is extremely important to not only understand the differences, but to be able to execute flawlessly, the two styles. Blues Swing is the primary style you hear in the Blues Shuffle, Boogie Woogie, Jazz Blues, and Slow Blues. Straight Blues is a faster, more driving style that you'll hear in Blues Rock (like Chuck Berry), Jump Blues, and Country Blues. Don't worry if you don't understand this concept right now; you will by the time you are done with the Guitarlele Blues Mastery book by Terry Carter.

Although the Guitarlele Blues Mastery book will focus on understanding the different styles of Blues through rhythm, it does explore other topics that I know you are interested in, such as Fingerstyle Blues, Blues Scales, and the Blues Solo. The Guitarlele Blues Mastery book is the most comprehensive book on Guitarlele and is written by Terry Carter, the leader in the Guitarlele world, youtube.com/ukelikethepros.

Whether you are a beginner at the Blues, or a seasoned veteran, the Guitarlele Blues Mastery book is going to take you deep into the world of the Blues, and you will come out a better, more confident guitarlele player, who will be ready to tackle the world.

Are you ready? Let's dive in.

Sounds Good?

It's now your turn to dive into the *Guitarlele Blues Mastery for Beginners*.

HISTORY OF THE BLUES

The Blues has a long history as an American artform dating back to the mid-1800's. The Blues was created out of African Spirituals that were born out of work songs or field songs. These songs were sung not only out of tradition, but to also help pass the time, and became the basis of the Blues that we know today. There are 3 keys parts you want to remember about the Blues:

1. Call & Response
This is the where one person or group would sing a phrase and then another person or group would respond to that phrase.

2. 12 Bar Blues Form
The 12 Bar Blues is the most common form for all Blues. Although some Blues can be 8 or even 16 bars long, the majority are 12 bars. This is a form you want to get down into your soul, so you know exactly where you are in the form of the 12 Bar Blues at any time.

3. Blues Scale
The main scale that is used to create Blues melodies, and to solo, come from the notes of the Blues Scale, which is the same as the Minor Pentatonic Scale, except that it has an added "Blue Note" in it (the b5 Note).

a. For example:
i. CALL – "When He Walks In The Joint"   ii. RESPONSE – "Everybody Turns To Look"

b. Call & Response can also happen between the voice and an instrument. B.B. King is famous for this, as he would sing a phrase (Call) and then answer it with his guitar (Response).

The Blues Scale in A would be:
A – C – D – Eb – E – G – A

BLUES FORM

The 12 Bar Blues form consists of 12 bars (or measures) that repeat over and over again and alternate between the I, IV, and V chords (usually seventh chords). If you are in the key of A, it would be called Blues in A, the I chord would be A7, the IV chord would be D7, and the V chord would be E7. In a 12 Bar Blues in A, bars 1-4 are played on the A7 chord, bars 5-6 on the D7, bars 7-8 return to the A7, bar 9 on the E7, and bar 10 on the D7. The last 2 bars (11-12) are called The Turnaround. Bar 11 returns to the A7 and bar 12 goes back to the E7 before it repeats.

12 Bar Blues in A

A7
1
2
3
4
D7
5
6
A7
7
8
E7
9
D7
10
A7
11
E7
12

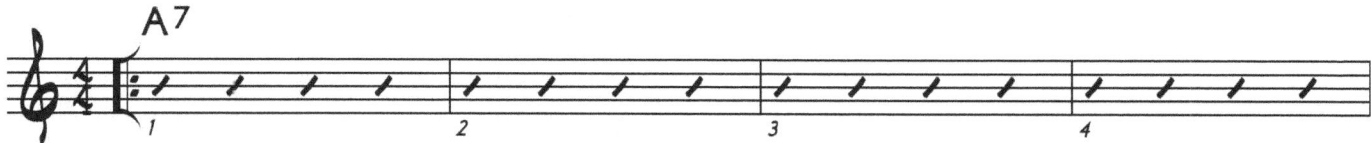

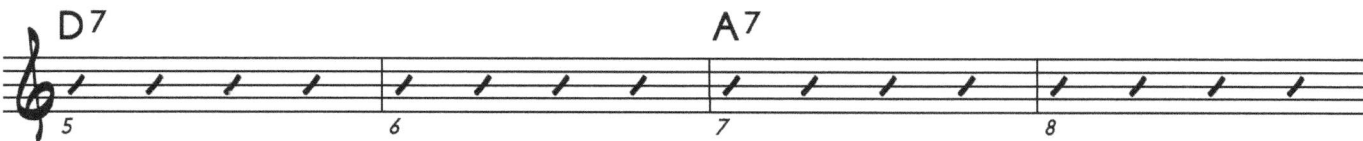

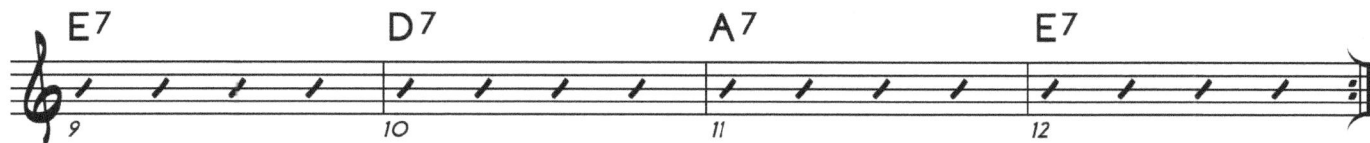

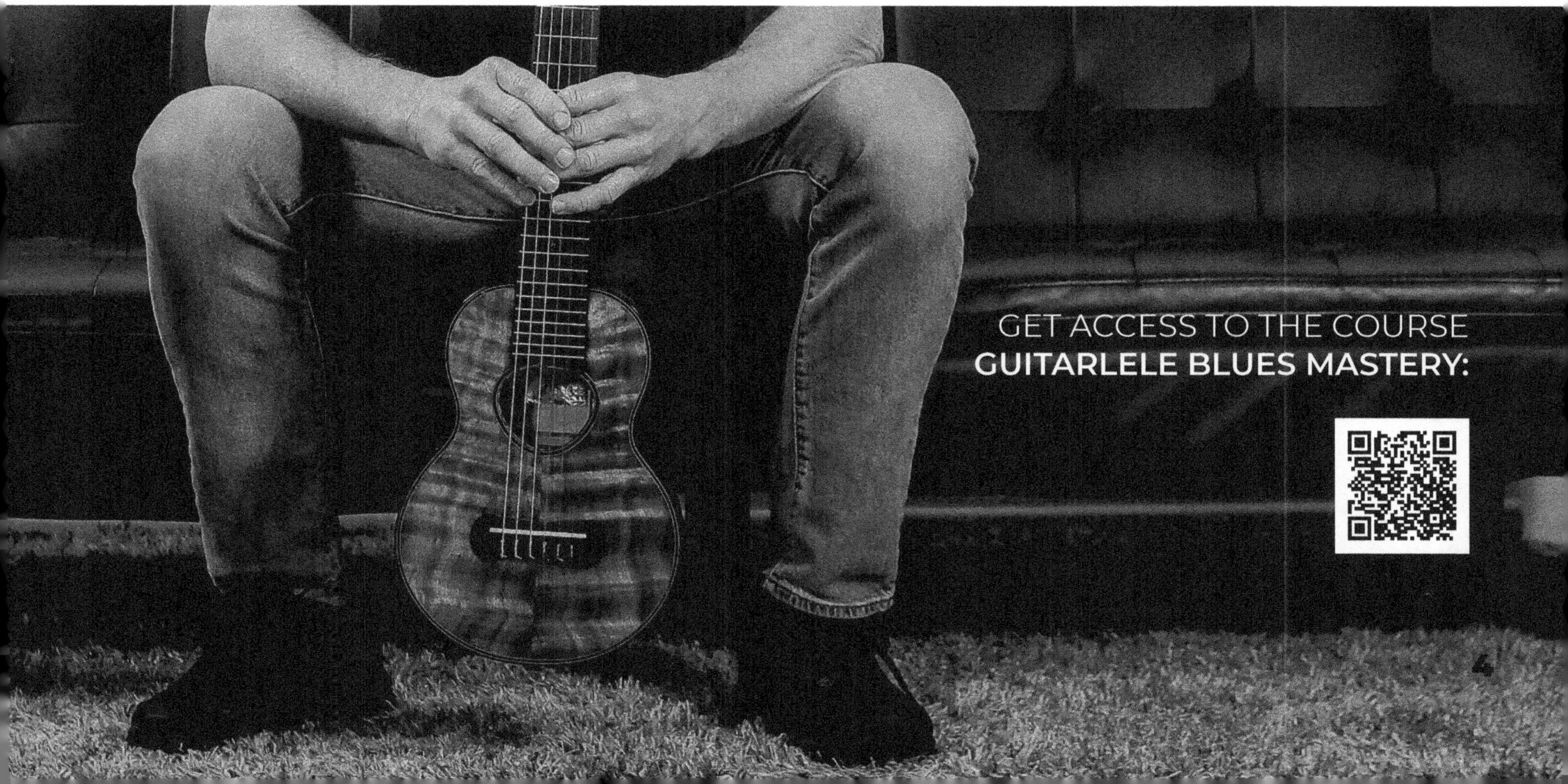

GET ACCESS TO THE COURSE
GUITARLELE BLUES MASTERY:

STRAIGHT VS SWING 1/8th NOTES

As a Blues Master it is absolutely necessary to be able to switch between playing swing 1/8th notes and straight 1/8 notes. Straight 1/8th notes are the easiest because all you have to do is divide the quarter note beat into 2 equal parts and count them 1 + 2 + 3 + 4 +. You'll hear straight 1/8th notes in Blues Rock, Country Blues, and Jump Blues.

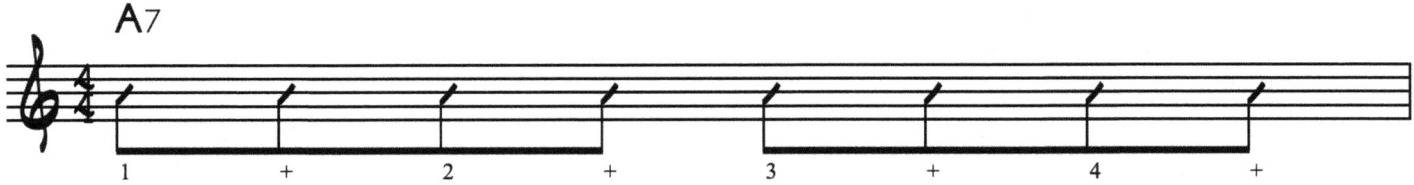

Swing 1/8th notes are a little harder to play and many times you'll hear people say, "just feel it." Although playing swing 1/8th notes is a feeling, you must understand how to divide the beat and play them properly. Let's start with a triplet, which is 3 notes per beat, and counted 1-trip-let, 2 trip-let, 3 trip-let, 4 trip-let.

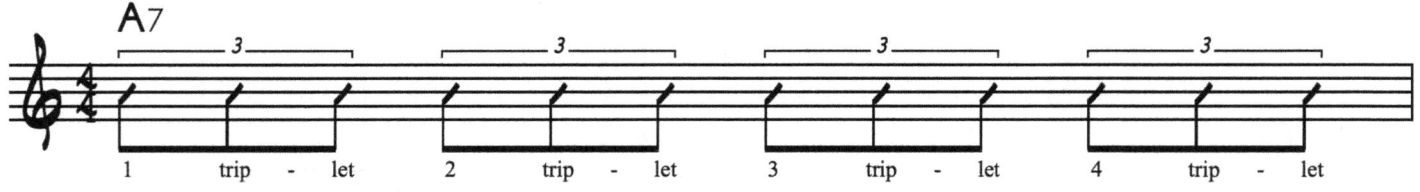

Now that you have mastered the triplets, to play Swing 1/8th notes simply play the first and the third note of each triplet, or don't play the middle note of the triplet "trip."

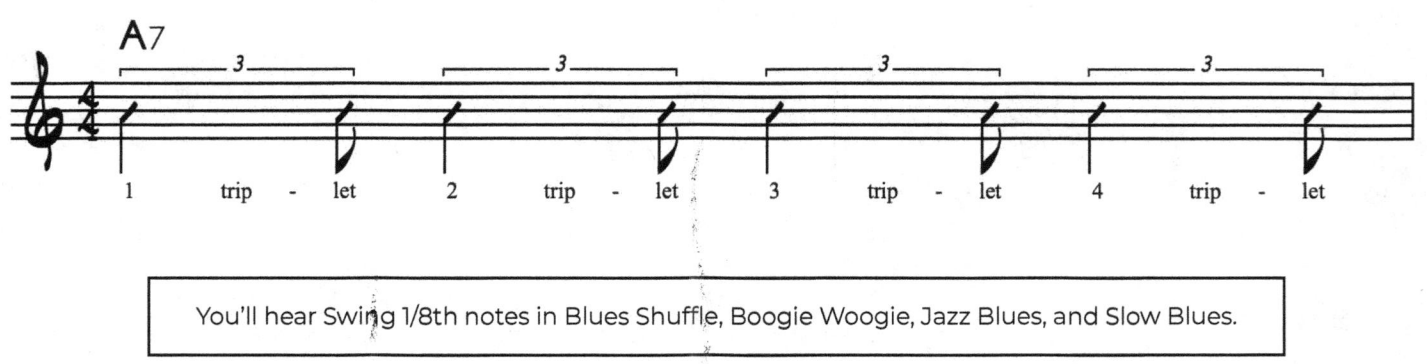

You'll hear Swing 1/8th notes in Blues Shuffle, Boogie Woogie, Jazz Blues, and Slow Blues.

HOW TO HOLD A PICK

Playing with a pick is totally acceptable on the guitarlele, and even recommended on certain songs. If you're a ukulele player, you might not have ever played with a pick, however if you're a guitar player chances are you have played with a pick. There are many different types of picks out there, made of different materials, thicknesses, and shapes. There is no right or wrong pick, it's simply the pick that feels comfortable and sounds pleasing to your style.
A good place to start is a Uke Like The Pros medium pick, available at store.ukelikethepros.com.

To hold the pick, grip it between your thumb and index finger. You need to grip it tight enough so that it doesn't slide around when you play, but not so tight that you are feeling strain in your fingers or wrists.
A good place to strum the guitarlele is halfway between the end of the fretboard and the bridge.
Most likely this will be towards the bottom of the soundhole.

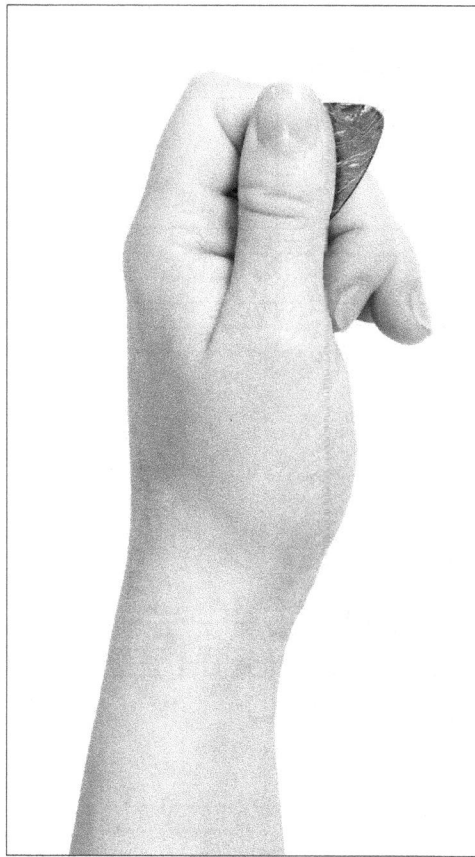 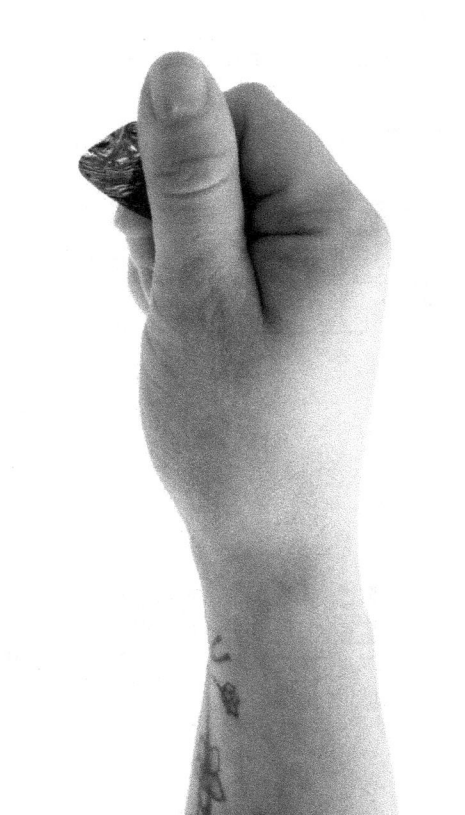 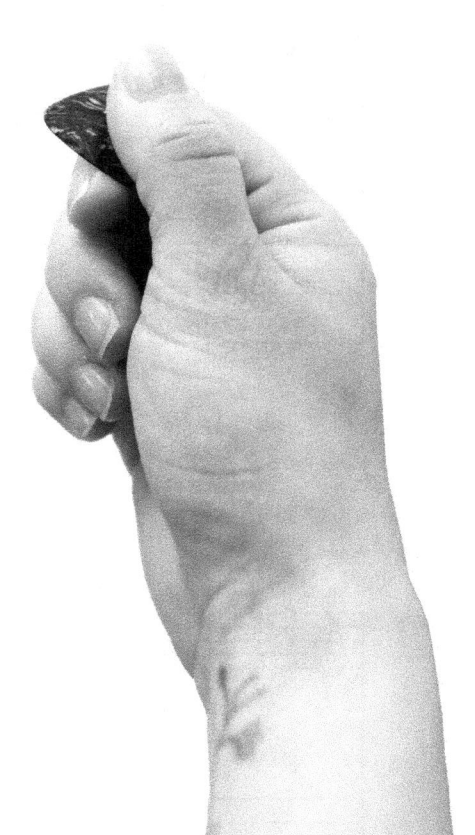

STRUMMING BLUES IN A

This lesson will be a traditional 12 Bar Blues form in "A" played with Swing 1/8th notes. This strum pattern will be a core rhythm that you can play over many types of Blues. The rhythm will be all Swing 1/8th notes with a tie going from the "+ of 2" to beat "3". This means that you strum all the beats using a down-up pattern, but you will not strum beat 3 because of the tie. The only chords you need for this Strumming Blues is A7, D7, and E7.

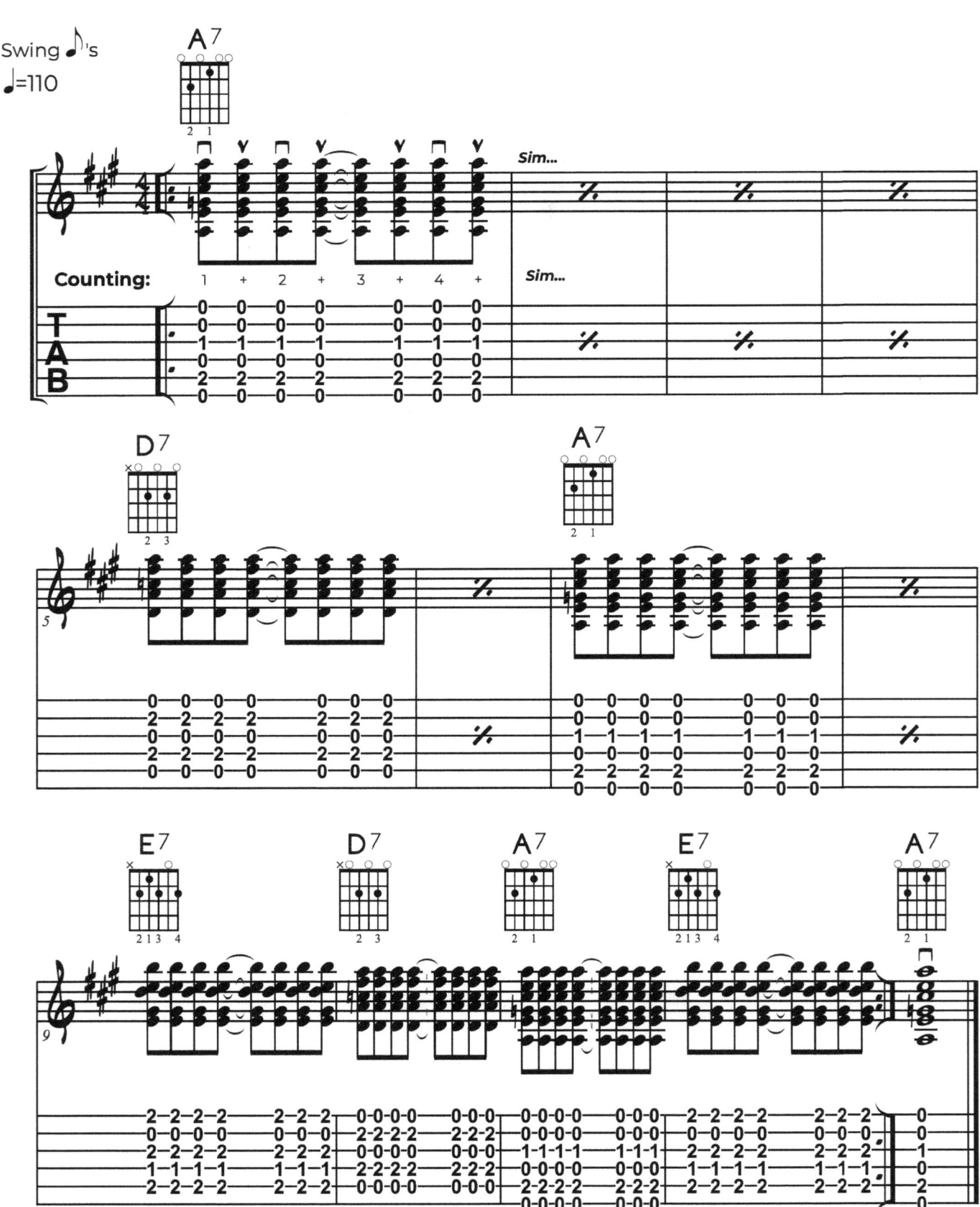

STRUMMING BLUES IN A *WITH QUICK-CHANGE*

Are you ready to be blown away? Good, because in this lesson you will learn the quick-change. A quick-change is so simple, yet extremely vital as a Blues player. This lesson is exactly the same as the Strumming Blues in A lesson, but it uses a quick-change. A quick-change is when you go to the IV chord in measure two. Since we are in the key of A the IV chord is the D7 chord, so the 1st four measures will be A7 – D7 – A7 – A7. Although it doesn't seem like much, it makes a big difference in the sound of the tune and will affect the vocal melody of any Blues tune.

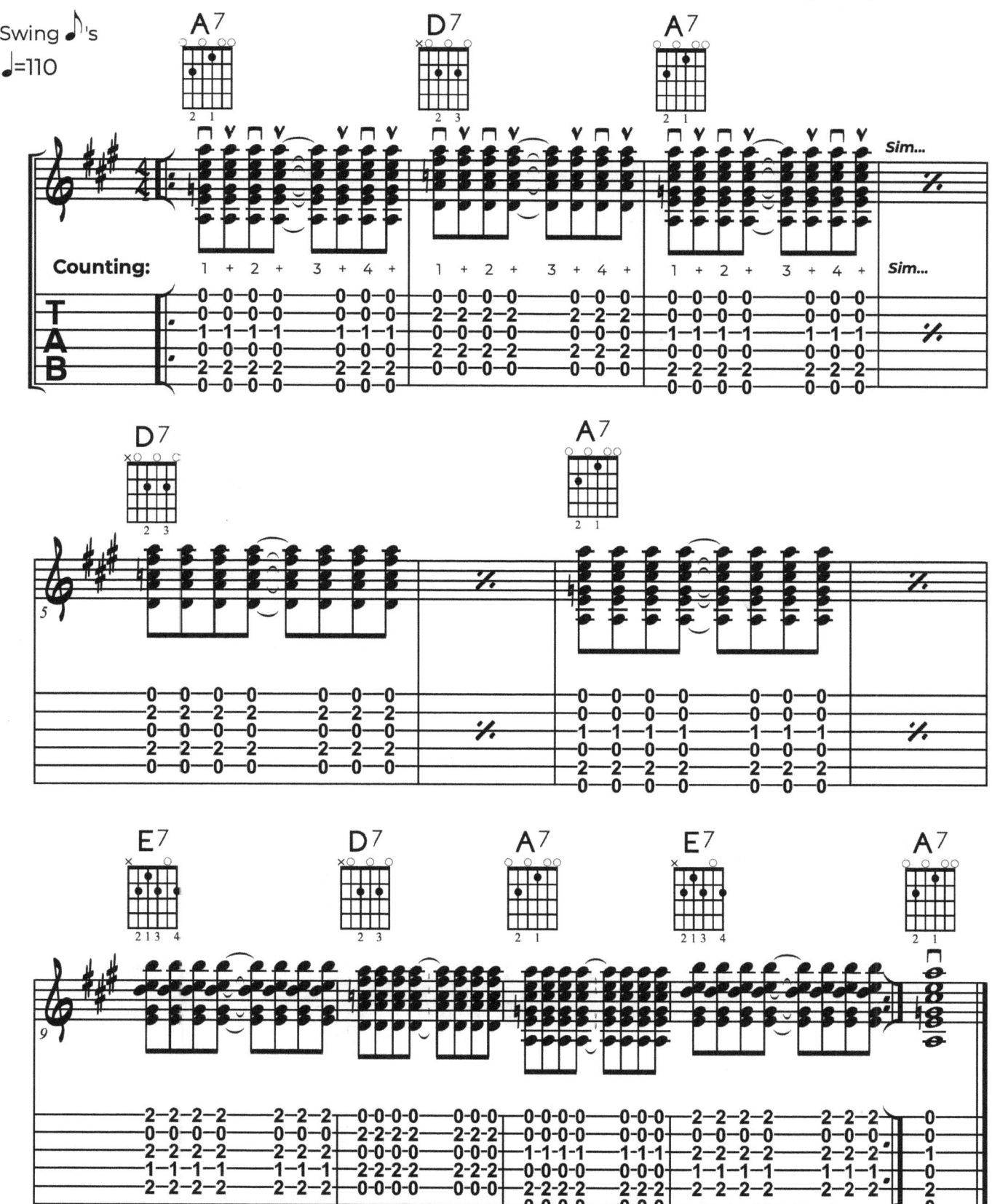

STRUMMING BLUES IN A *WITH MUTES*

We are going to continue with the same strum pattern as the previous lessons, but we are going to add mutes. We will be using the quick-change in this lesson but adding muted strums on beat 2 and beat 4. In the music the mutes are indicated by "x." This mute is done with the palm of your strumming hand and can be referred to as palm muting or "chucking." To get the mute, the side of your strumming palm is going to lightly touch all the strings an instant before you strum the strings. Mutes may feel awkward at first but will be smoother with practice.

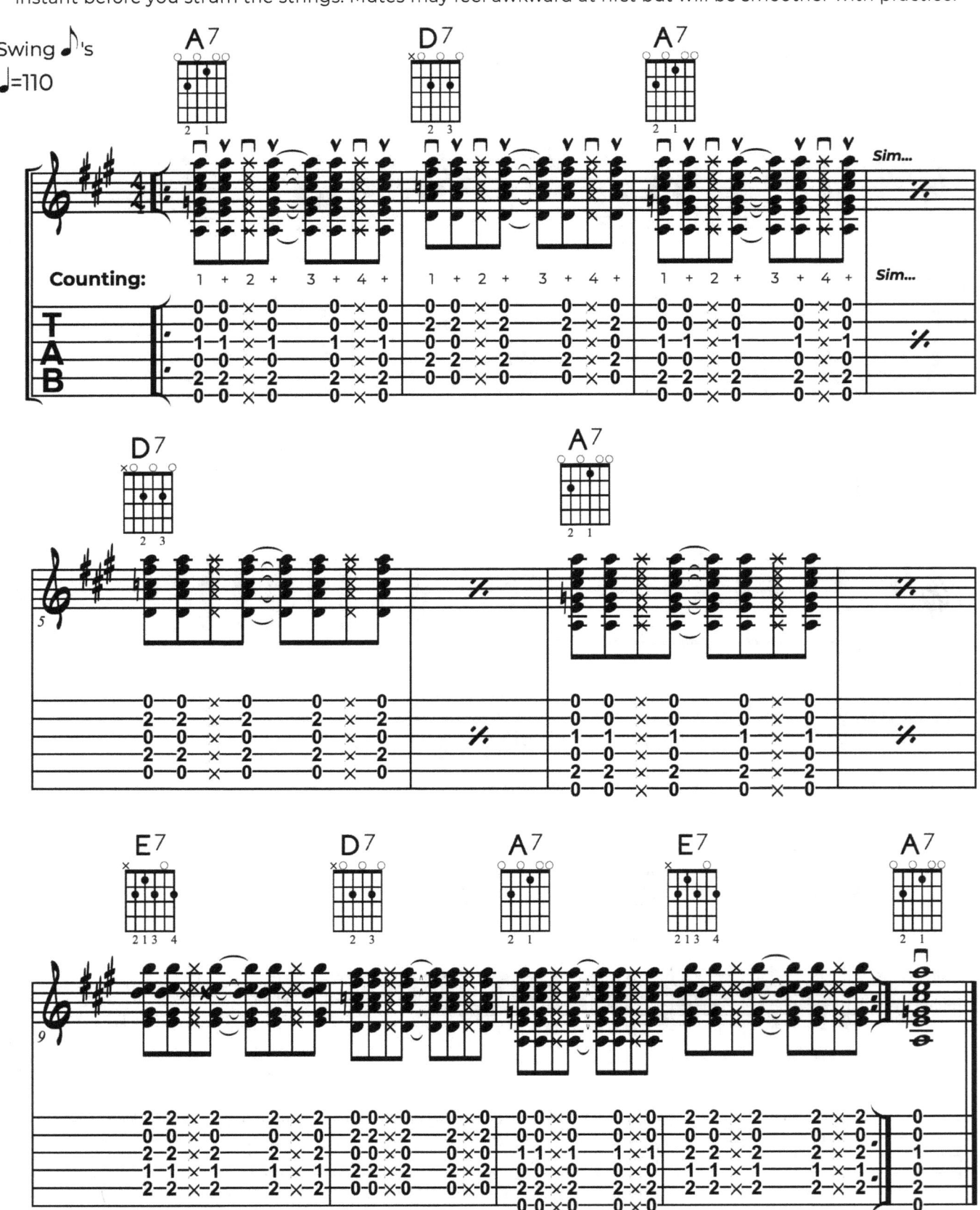

WALKING THE BLUES IN A

Up to this point you have been working on strumming, but let's play a Blues with all single notes. In this Walking The Blues lesson, you will play a cool single note pattern that will not only sound cool but be a great technique builder as well. You can play this lesson with all downstrokes with your thumb, like I do I the accompanying video course at ukelikethepros.com/guitarleleblues (sold separately), or with a pick. If you use a pick make sure to use an alternating down-up picking pattern. Practice it slowly and follow the fretting fingering that is under the TAB.

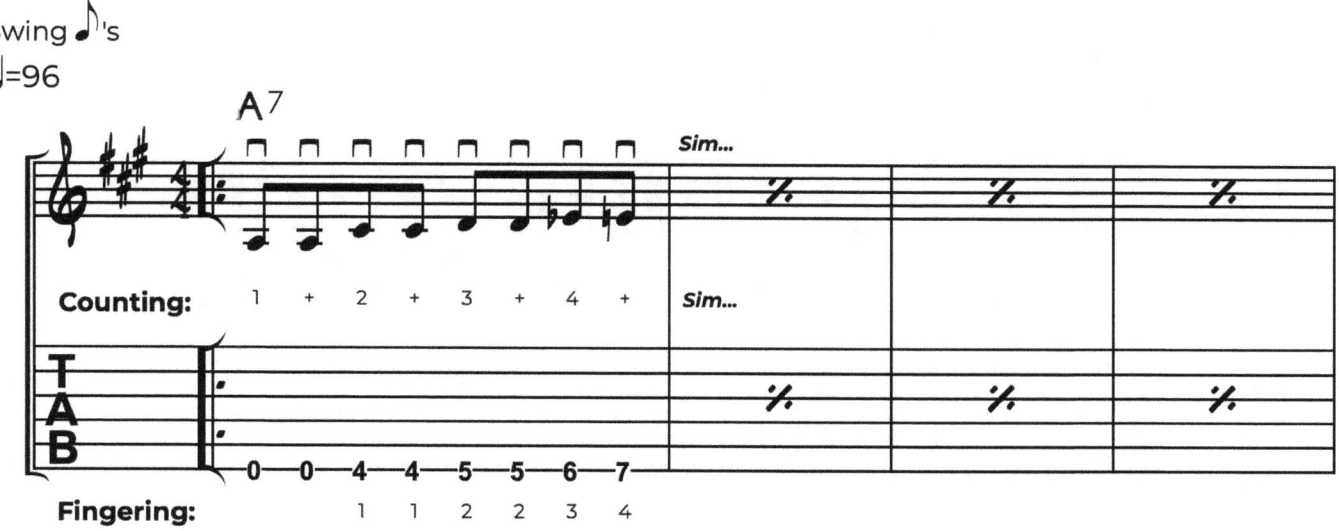

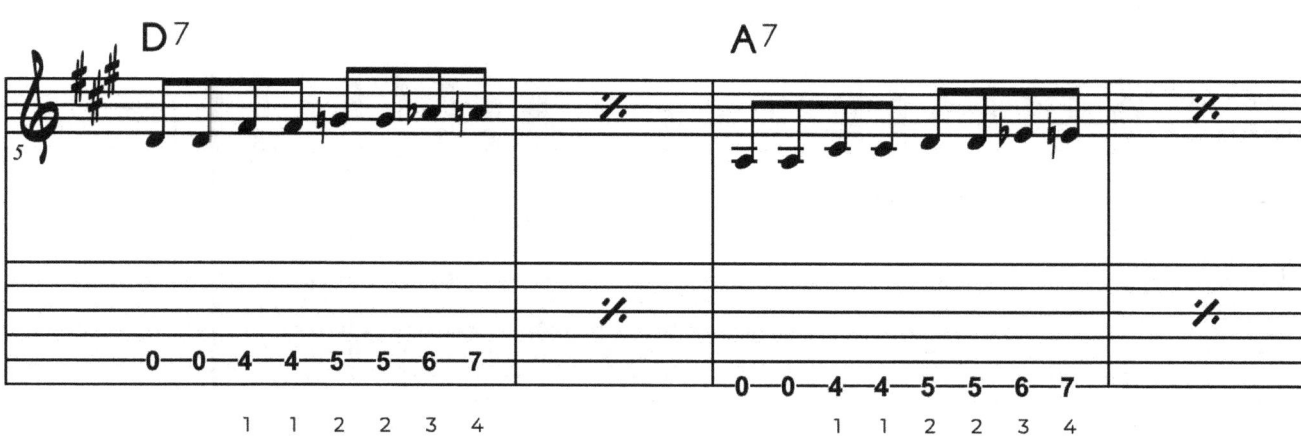

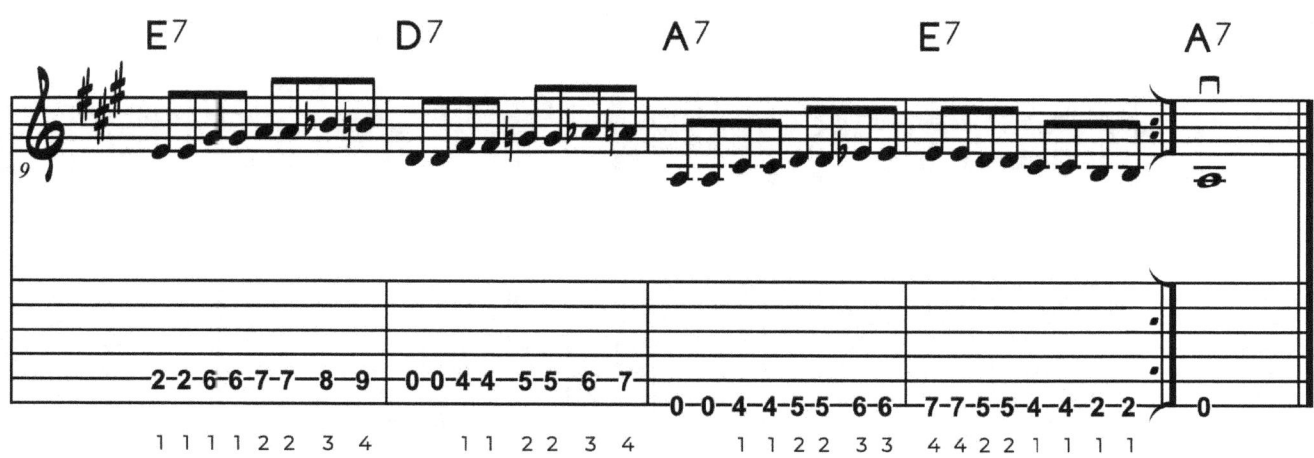

BOOGIE WOOGIE IN A *OPEN CHORDS*

This lesson will take what you learned in the Strumming Blues but take it up a step by adding some moving notes to each open chord. By simply adding these moving notes on beats 2 and 4, you create a style called Boogie Woogie. This Boogie Woogie sound is something that was taken from piano players and adapts very well to guitarlele.

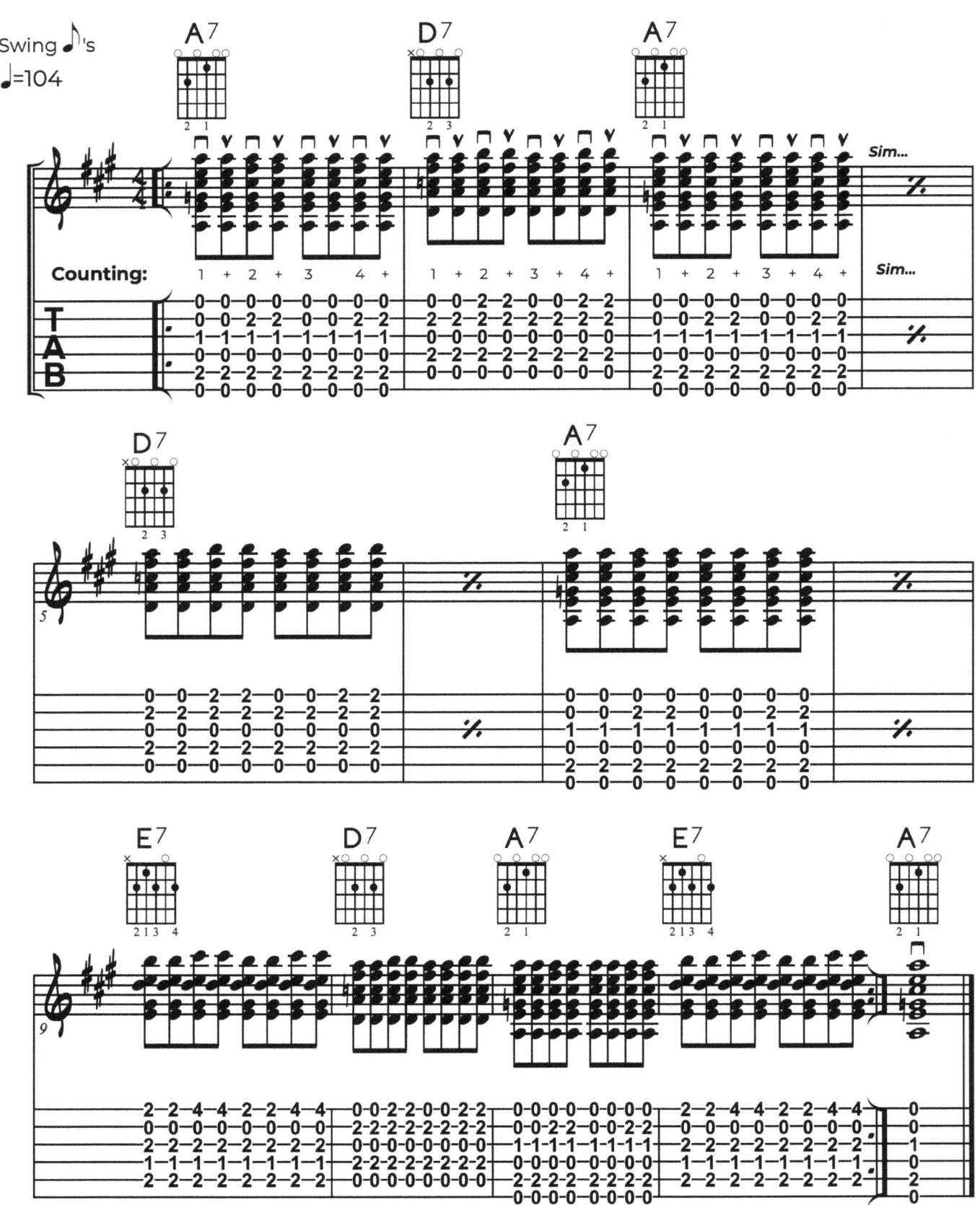

BOOGIE WOOGIE IN A *POWER CHORDS*

Now it's time to step up your Blues playing. Instead of using open position chords, we are going to use 2-string power chords. The A and the D chords are open power chords (at least one open string), but the E chord will be a closed power chord (no open strings) and will stretch your fingers a bit and require more strength. The benefit to using power chords is that they give you more of a driving powerful sound. Also, this lesson will teach you the coolest Blues Turnaround (bars 11-12) using single note triplets. Triplets are when you play 3 notes in one beat.

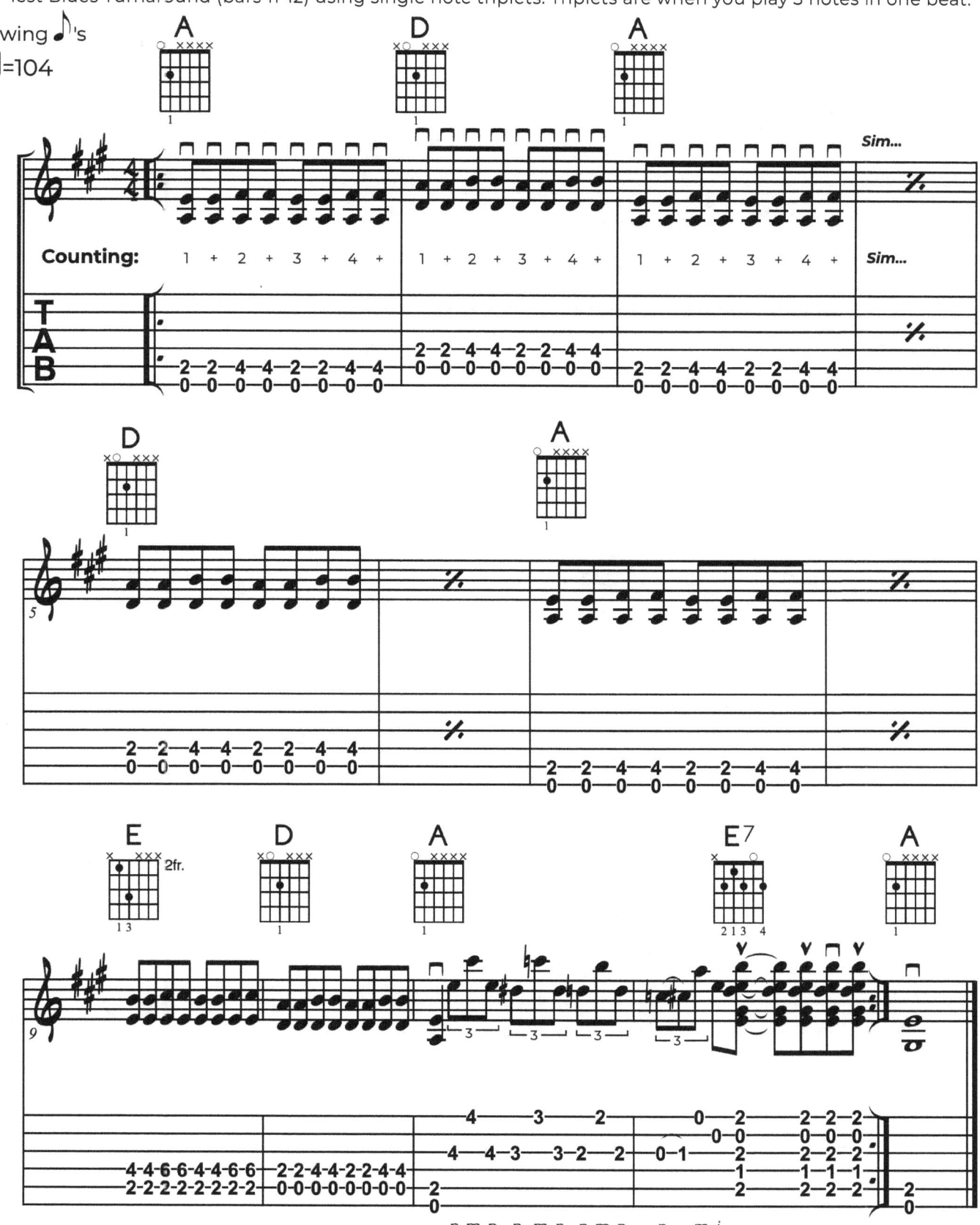

BOOGIE WOOGIE IN B *CLOSED POWER CHORDS*

By taking the A power chord and moving it up 2 frets, you get the key of B. The chords in the key of B are all closed power chords and will give us the B, E, and F# power chords. The B power chord will be on the 6th string 2nd fret, the E will be on the 5th string 2nd fret, and the F# will be on the 5th string 4th fret. The power chords are a great way to not only build up your technique, but also are really useful when you start playing Blues Rock in the style of greats such as Chuck Berry.

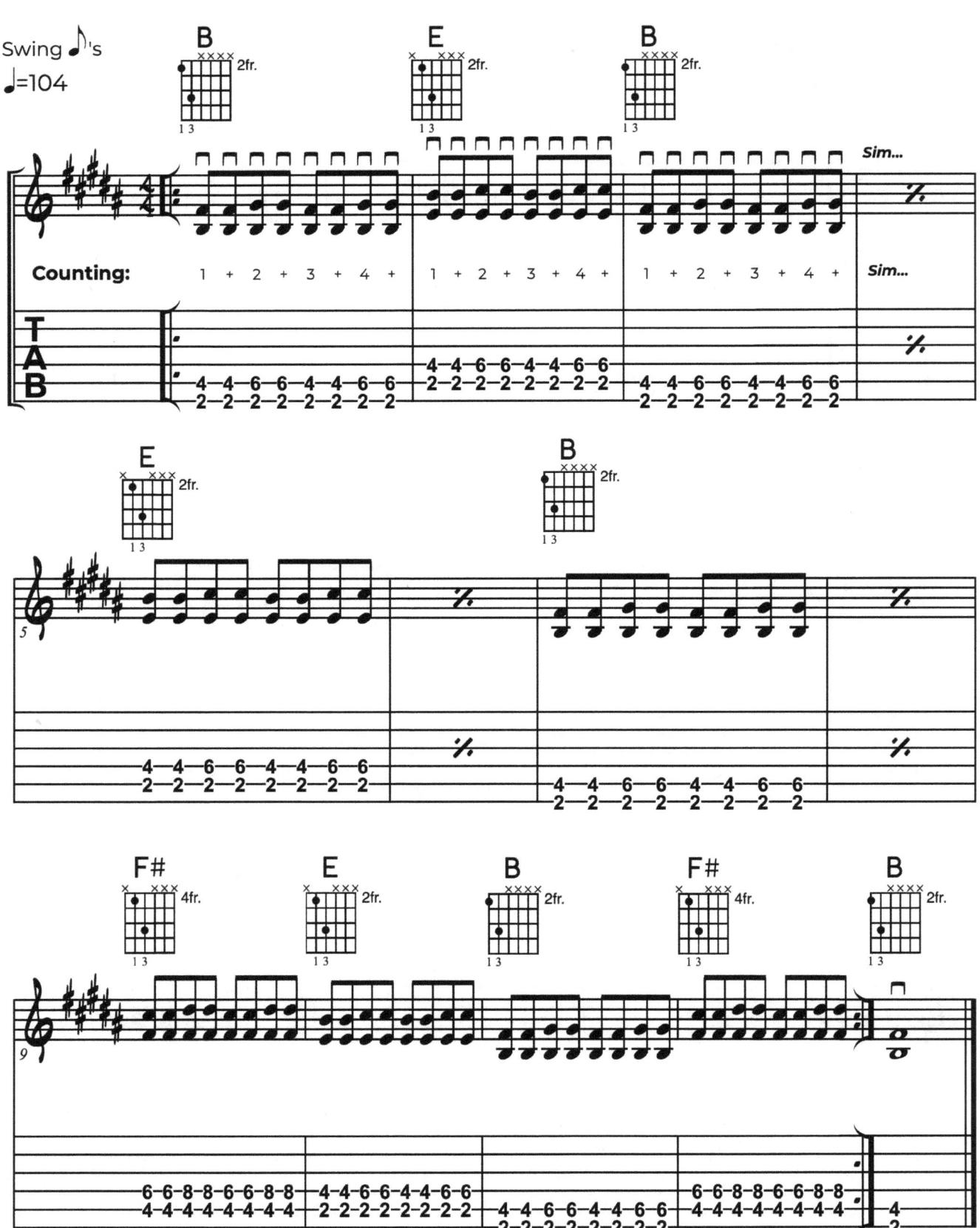

FINGERSTYLE BLUES IN A

This will be a Blues in A with a twist. The twist is that we are going to play this piece fingerstyle with straight 1/8th notes and use a hip turnaround. The turnaround goes A7 – D7 – A7 – E7 with each chord getting 2 beats. You'll be playing a unique fingerstyle pattern that is going to use all four fingers of your picking hand: p (thumb), i (index), m (middle), and a (ring) fingers. Although this pattern may take you a bit to master, it is a pattern that really works for this song which has a Country/Americana vibe to it.

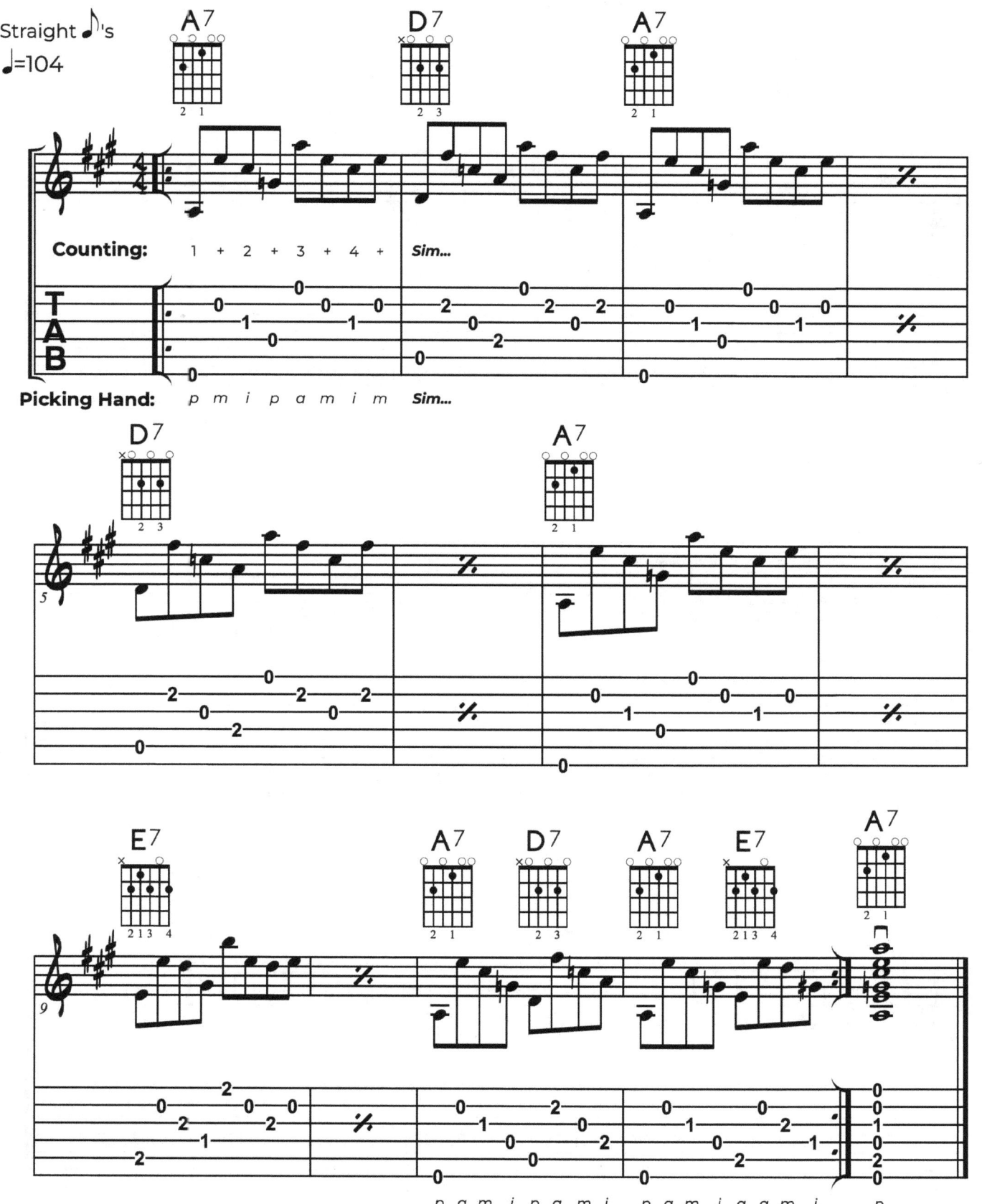

BLUES ROCK IN A

Chuck Berry anyone? Did you know that the early Rock and Roll stars, such as Chuck Berry and Elvis took the slower Blues Shuffle and sped it up, played straight 1/8th notes, and added fun lyrics about cars, love, and partying to create Rock and Roll? It's true. Even though Rock and Roll borrowed from R & B (Rhythm & Blues), Country, and Pop music in the 1950's, it took the most from Rhythm & Blues. This piece is in the key of A and will go back to the open position power chords, but by playing straight 1/8th notes it creates a driving Johnny G. Goode rock sound.

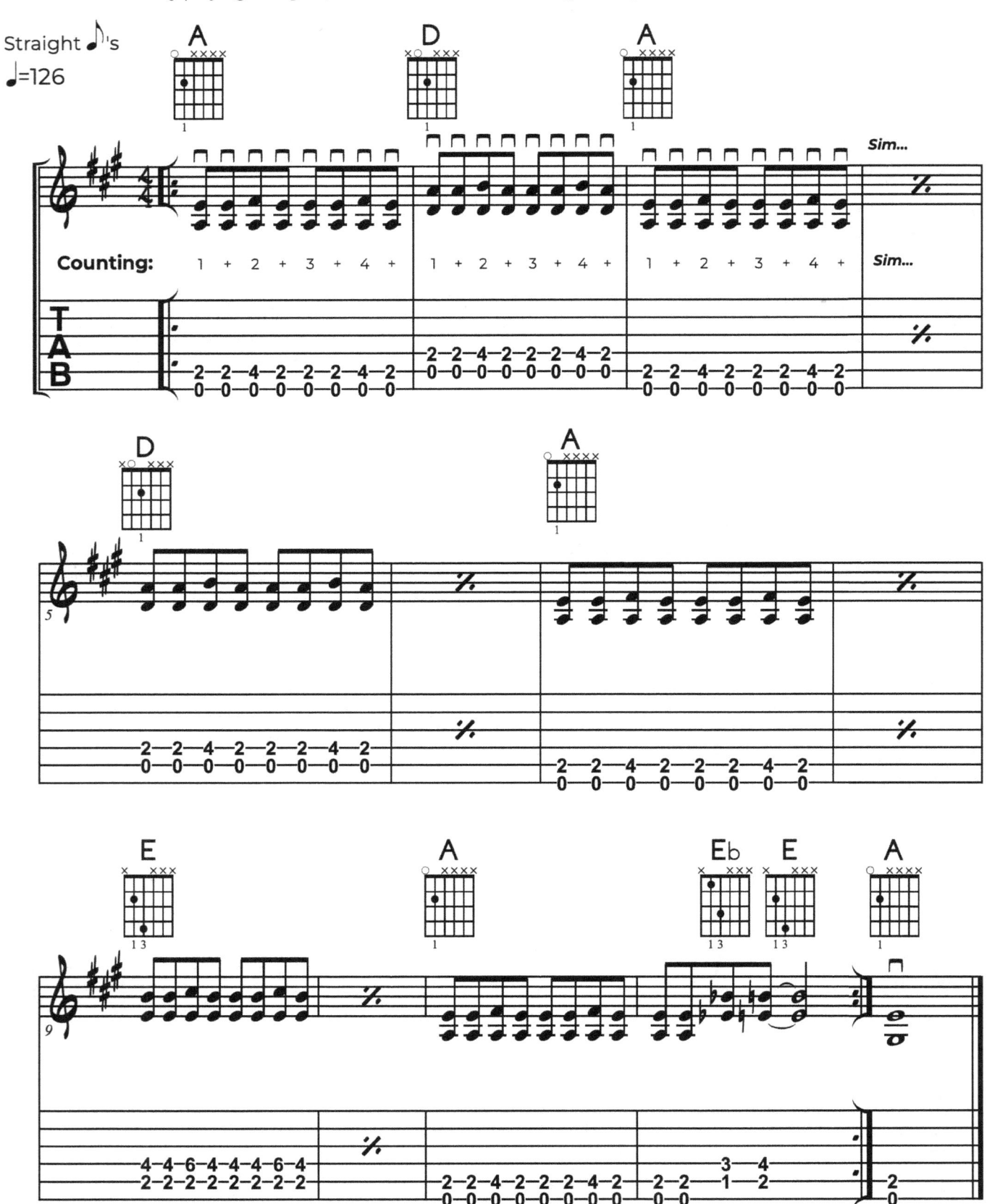

BLUES ROCK IN B

Just like in the Boogie Woogie lessons, we can transpose the Blues Rock style to any key. By moving all the power chords from A up 2 frets we get the Key of B. The key of B will give you the I, IV, V chords that are B, E, and F#. You'll play this one with straight 1/8th notes and use a quick change. Also measure 12 has a ½ step slide that goes from F to F# on beat 2 to give the piece a fresh sounding turnaround.

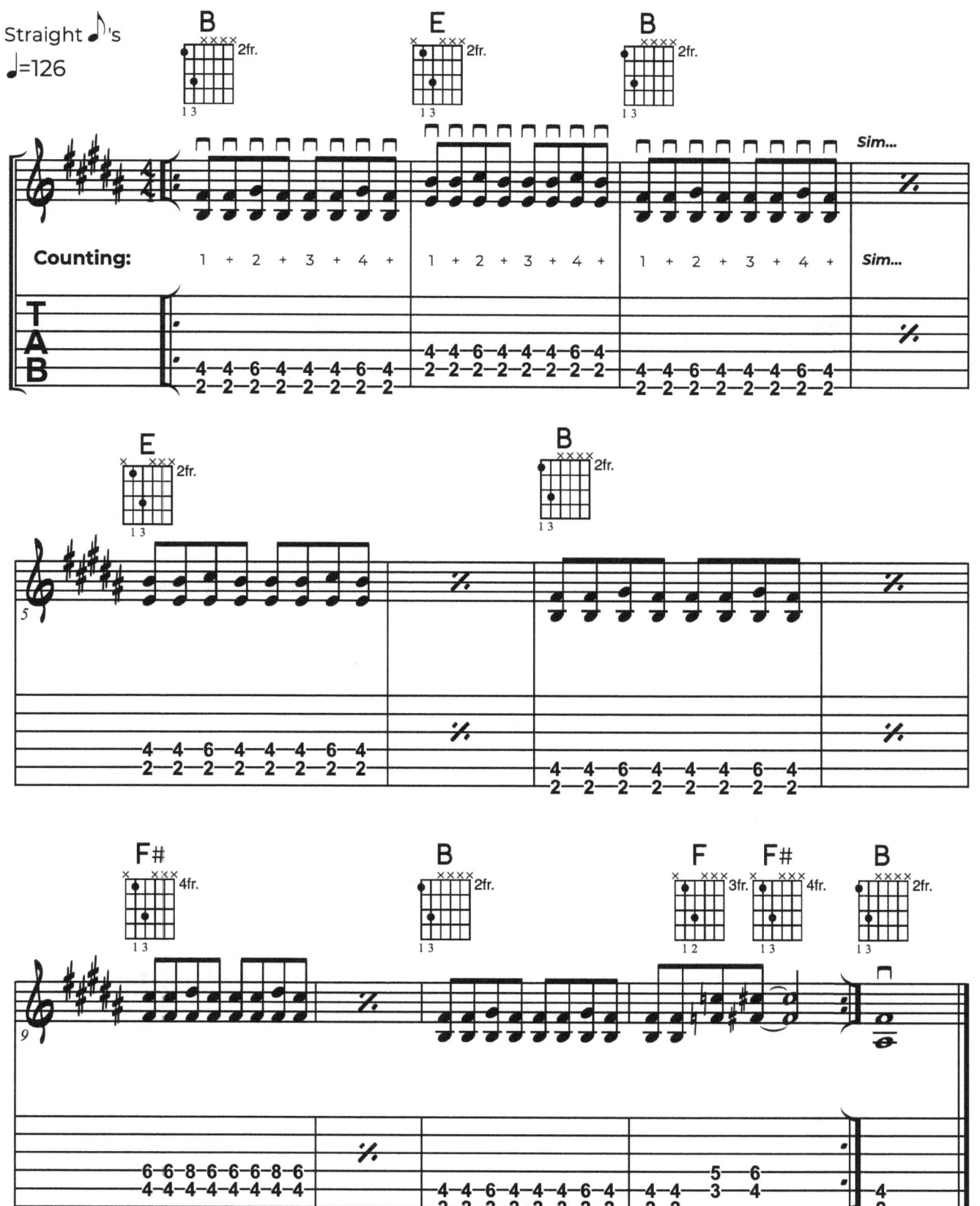

JUMP BLUES IN A
PG. 1 of 2

Are you ready to be blown away? For this Jump Blues you are going to continue playing straight 1/8th notes, but it will weave between single notes and chord strums. The single notes are a 2-bar walking bass pattern that can be played with a pick using up-down alternate picking. The strum pattern will be the same pattern we used back in the Strumming Blues in A with Mutes lesson. You will notice that the last 4 bars use all single notes and no strumming. We will use a 1st and 2nd ending (play the 1st ending the 1st time and after you repeat skip the 1st ending and play the 2nd ending) that will end in the climactic A7#9 chord. The A7#9 chord is also known as the Jimi Hendrix chord, as he used it in songs such as Purple Haze.

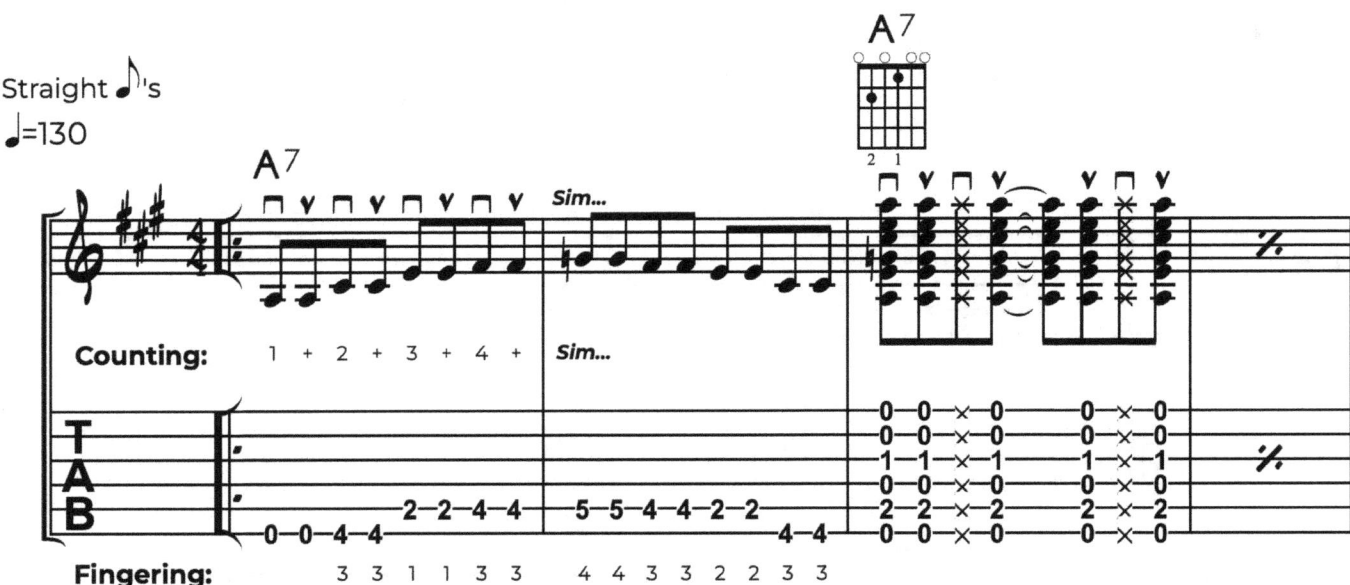

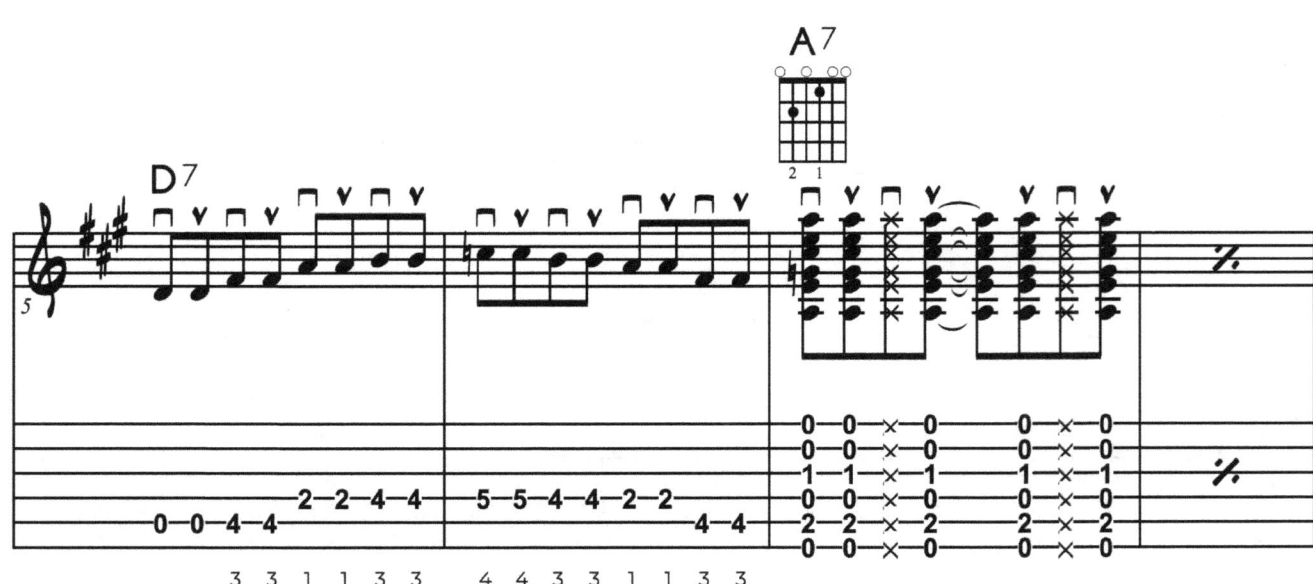

JUMP BLUES IN A
PG. 2 of 2

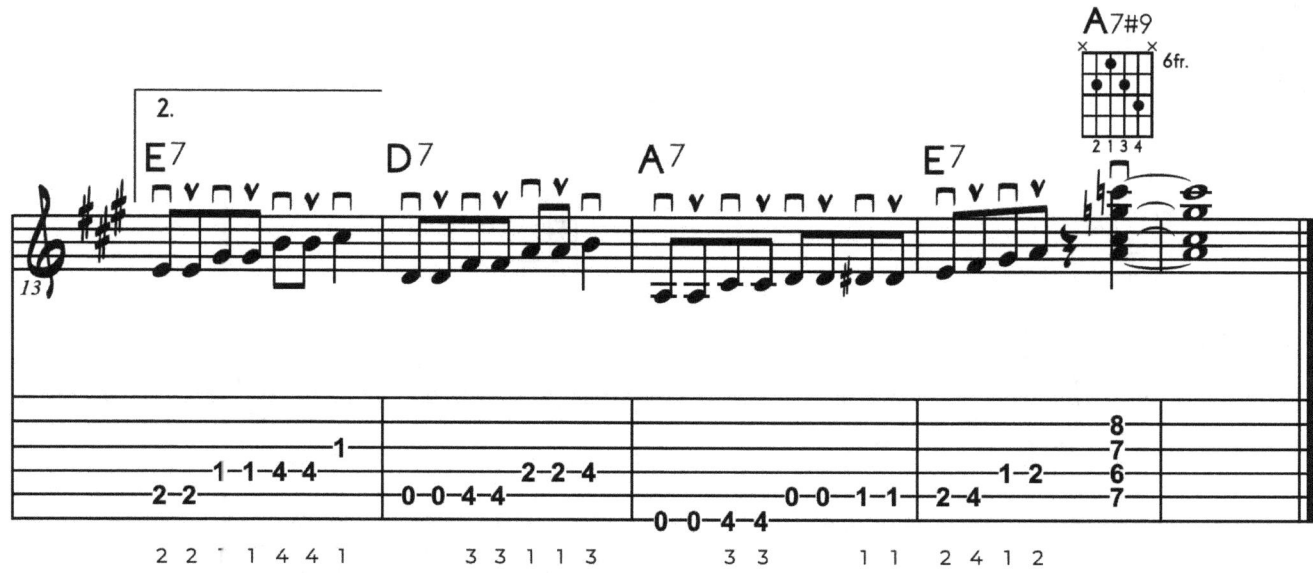

INTERESTED IN **GUITAR**?
ONLINE COURSES:

COUNTRY BLUES IN A

If Johnny Cash were with us today, he would play a strum pattern like this. This is known as the Bass Strum pattern, because on beats 1 and 3 you will be playing a bass note, and on beats 2 and 4 you will use a down-up strum pattern. You'll notice that the bass notes alternate between the root and the 5th of each chord. For example, on the A chord you will play the A bass note (open 6th string) on beat 1 and then you will play the 5th degree of the A chord which is the E bass note (5th string, 2nd fret) on beat 3. This moving bass captures the essence of what Classic Country is all about.

SLOW 12/8 BLUES IN A

PG. 1 of 2

The Slow 12/8 Blues can be heard in songs such as Stormy Monday by T-Bone Walker and the Allman Brothers. The 12/8 means 12 1/8th notes per measure. This Blues has a jazzy sound adding more than just the I, IV, and V chords you normally see in a Blues. The things you'll notice are the addition of 1/2 step slides (A7 to Bb7), walk ups (A7 - Bmin& - C#min7 - Cmin7), Minor 7th chords, and the E7+ chord (aka E7 augmented or #5 chord).

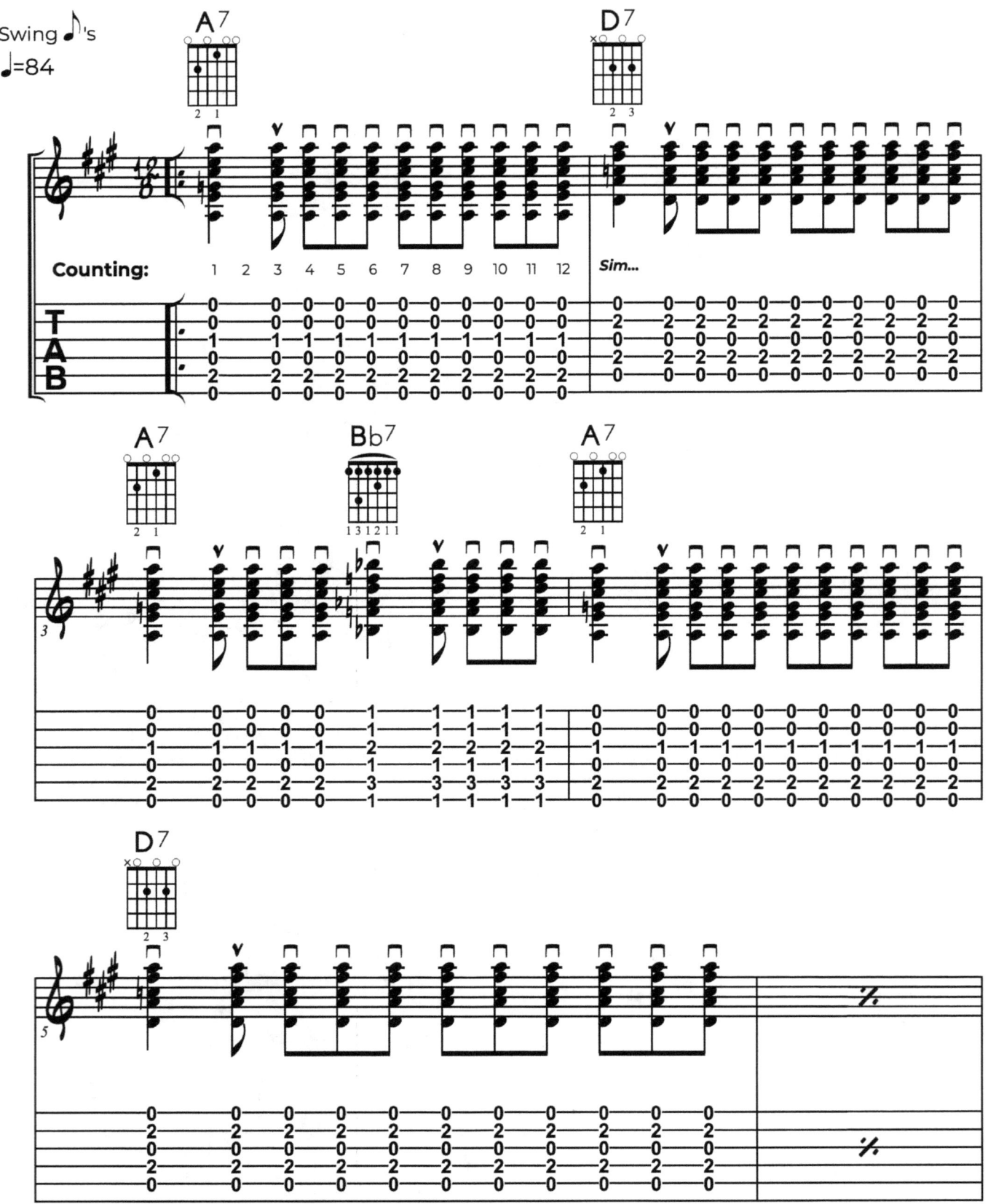

SLOW 12/8 BLUES IN A

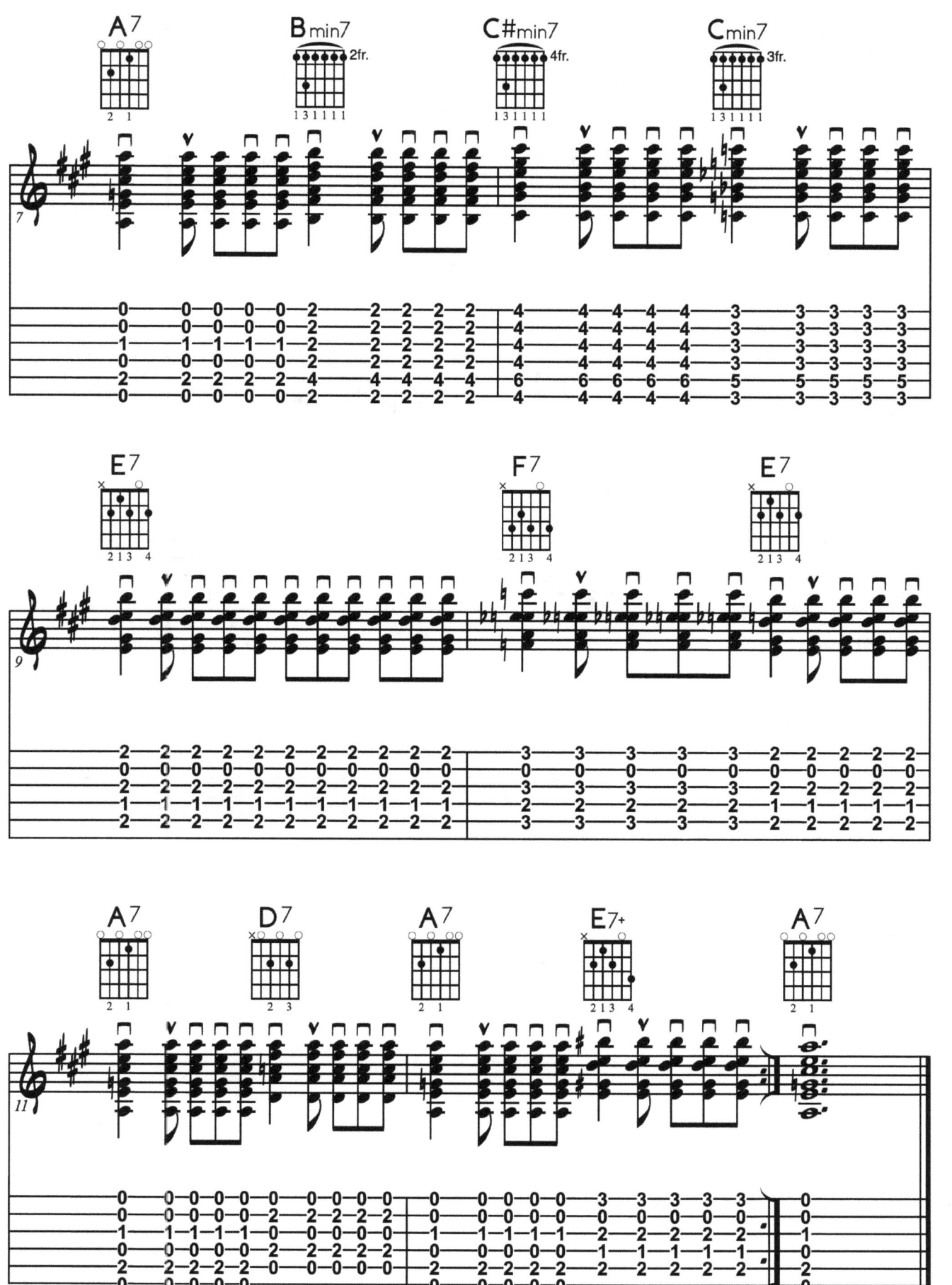

BLUES SCALE IN A

The Blues Scale is the most widely used and important scales used in the Blues, as it forms the foundation for Blues melodies and soloing. The Minor Pentatonic is another important scale, but if you can play the Blues Scale, you can play the Minor Pentatonic Scale since the Blues Scale only adds one additional note, the flat 5 (b5). The notes of the Blues Scale in A are A – C – D – Eb – E – G. For this lesson you will learn a 2 ½ octave Blues Scale in A that start from open 6th string (an A note) and go all the way up to the 7th fret (an E note) of the first string. Make sure to memorize this scale to get it in your fingers and ear. It would be easier to memorize the scale ascending first before tackling the descending part.

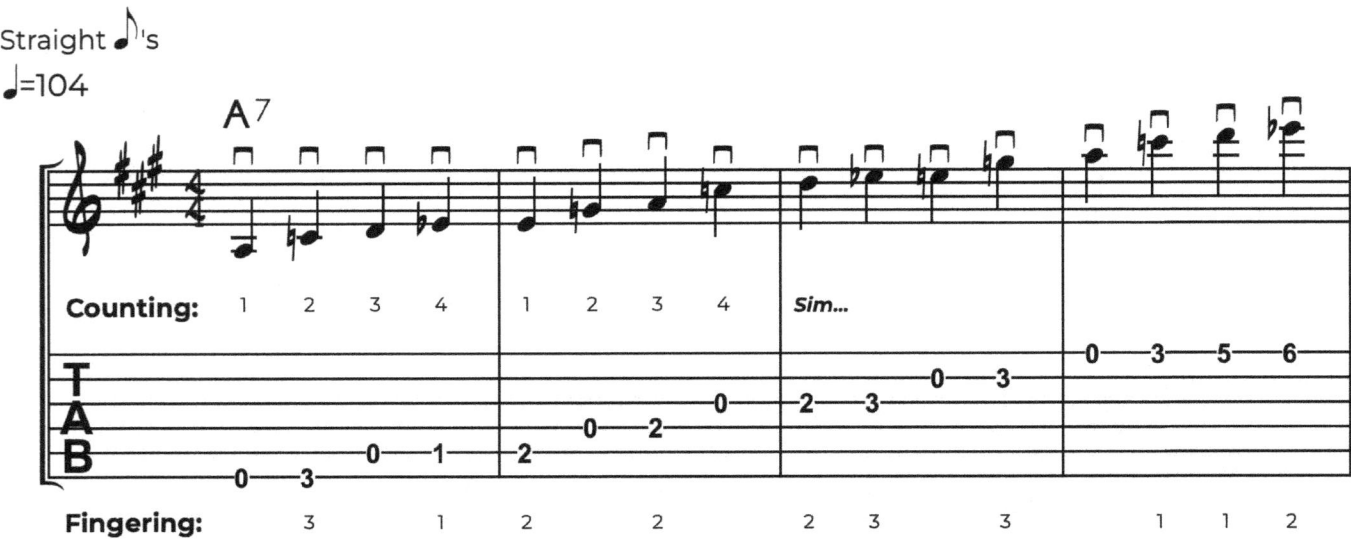

BLUES SOLO IN A
PG. 1 of 3

It's time to put everything together and learn your first solo. This solo uses a combination of the strum patterns you have been working on and licks from the Blues Scale. Licks are short musical phrases that are taken from the scale. To make the solo sound more authentic, you will be playing Slides (sliding from one note to another), Bends (where you bend a note up to a higher pitch), and Hammer On's (play a note and then "hammer" your finger onto another note without picking that note). You will also play some cool double stops (two notes at a time) in the turnaround section. One of the challenges you will face in this piece is switching from the strumming to the single notes. The cool thing about this piece is that it will sound great as a solo piece even if you're playing by yourself. Take it slow and crush it.

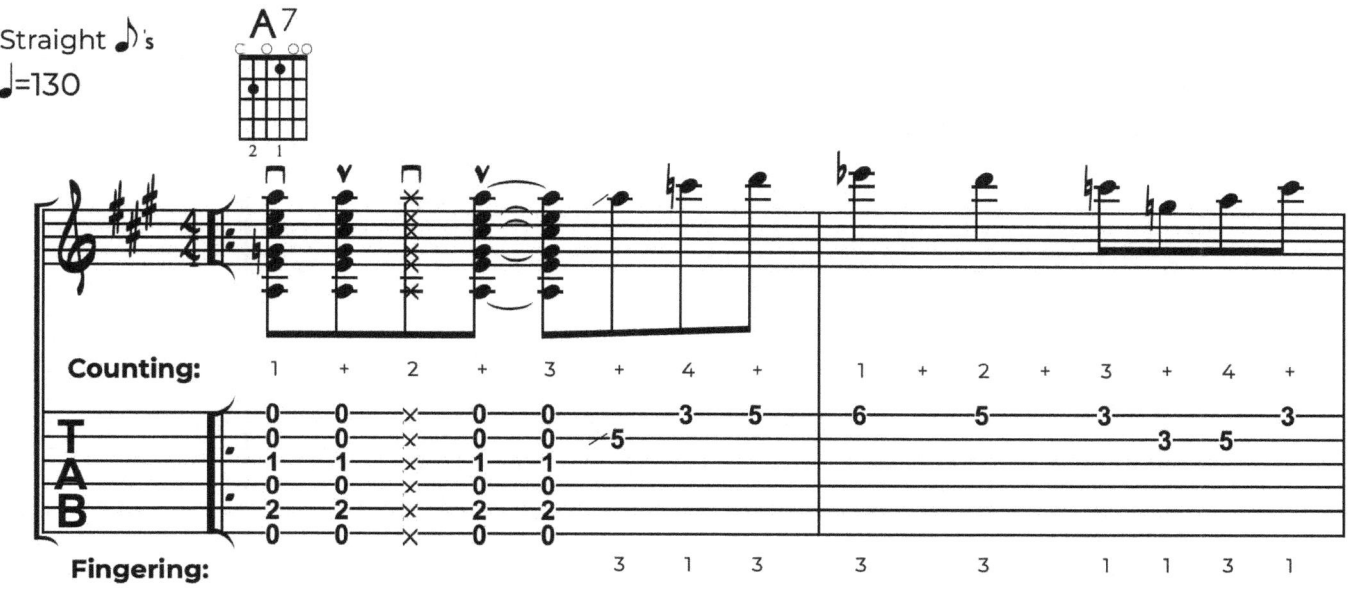

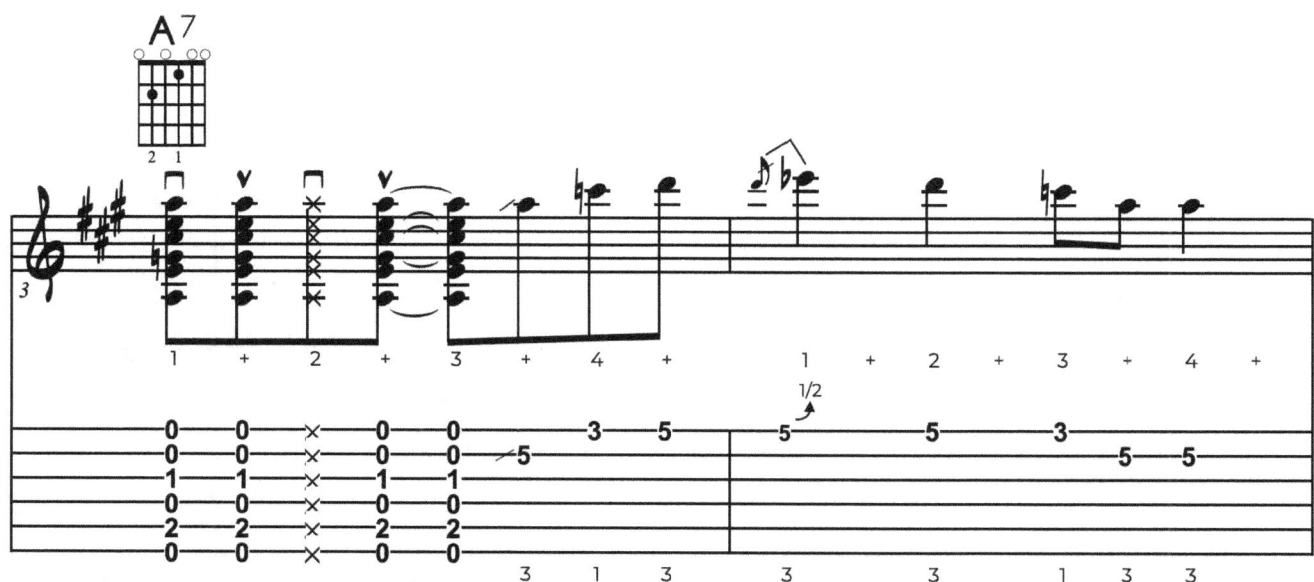

BLUES SOLO IN A
PG. 2 of 3

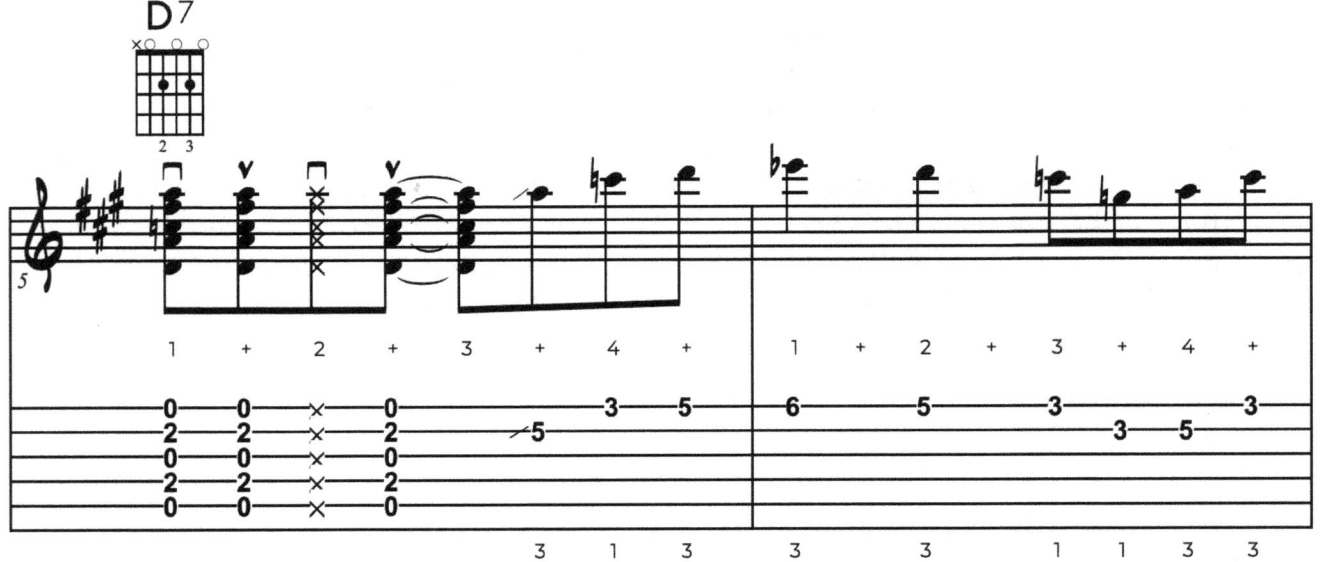
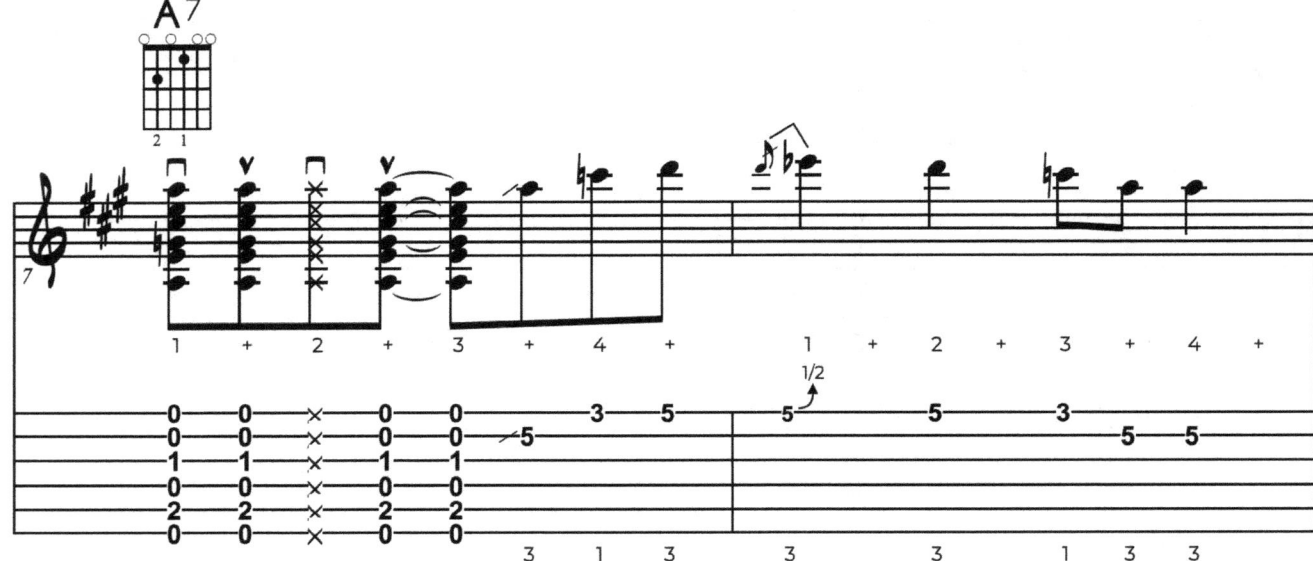
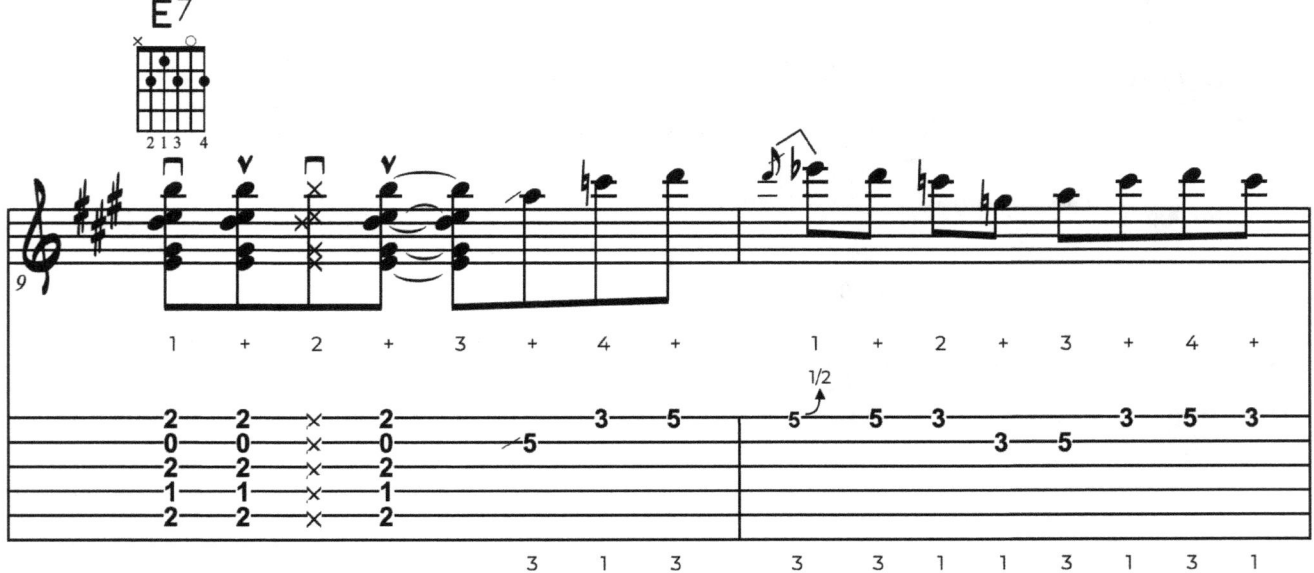

BLUES SOLO IN A
PG. 3 of 3

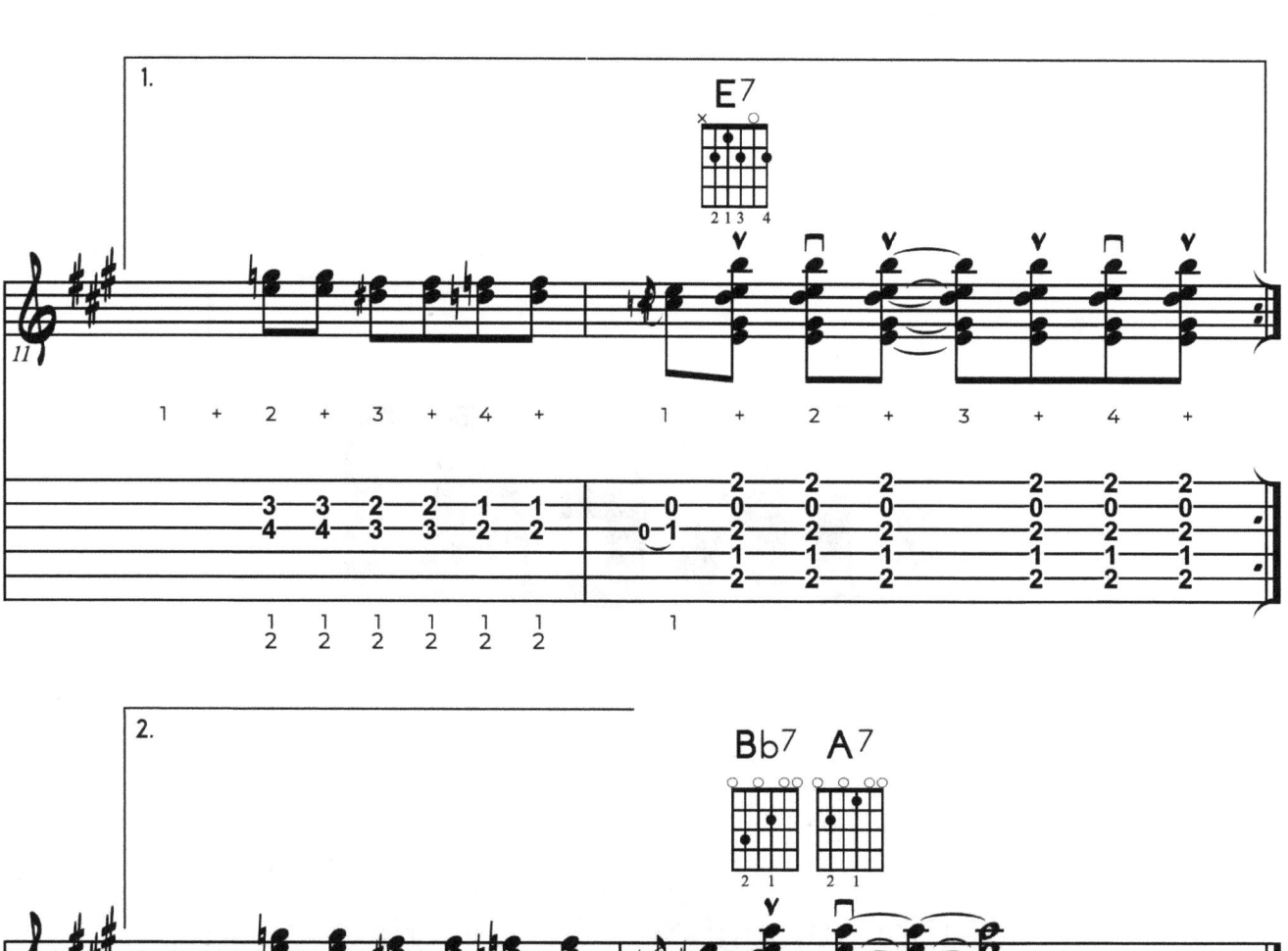

GREAT JOB!

I want to congratulate you for getting through the Guitarele Blues Mastery book by Uke Like The Pros and written by Terry Carter. You have learned a lot in this course and should now have a better understanding of the Blues, be a better guitarlele player, have better time, and be more confident. If you are interested in more guitarlele content, we have other guitarlele courses and content at **ukelikethepros.com**

THE ESSENTIALS

It is important to learn and memorize these terms and symbols because they not only apply to ukulele but to all music.

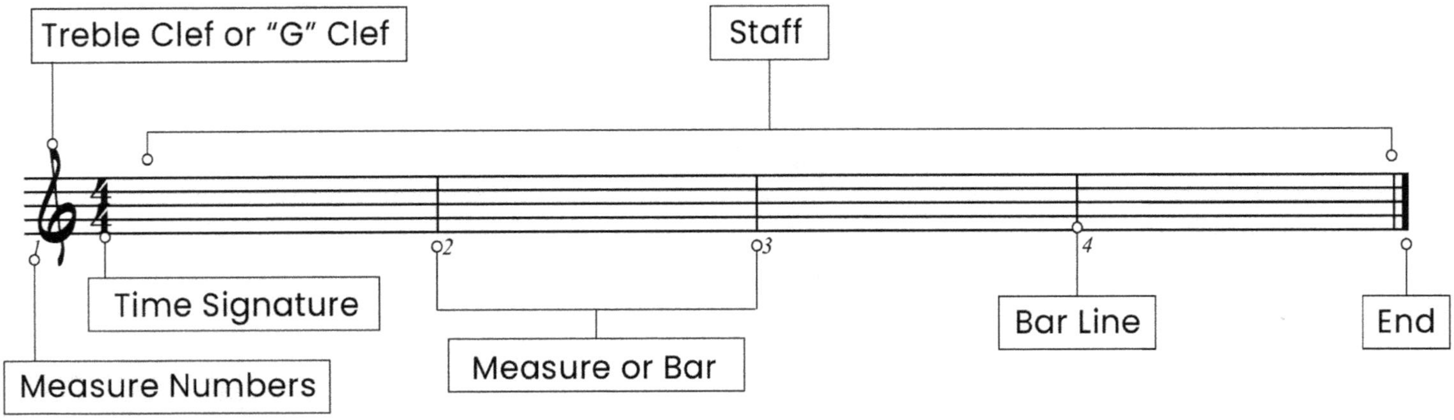

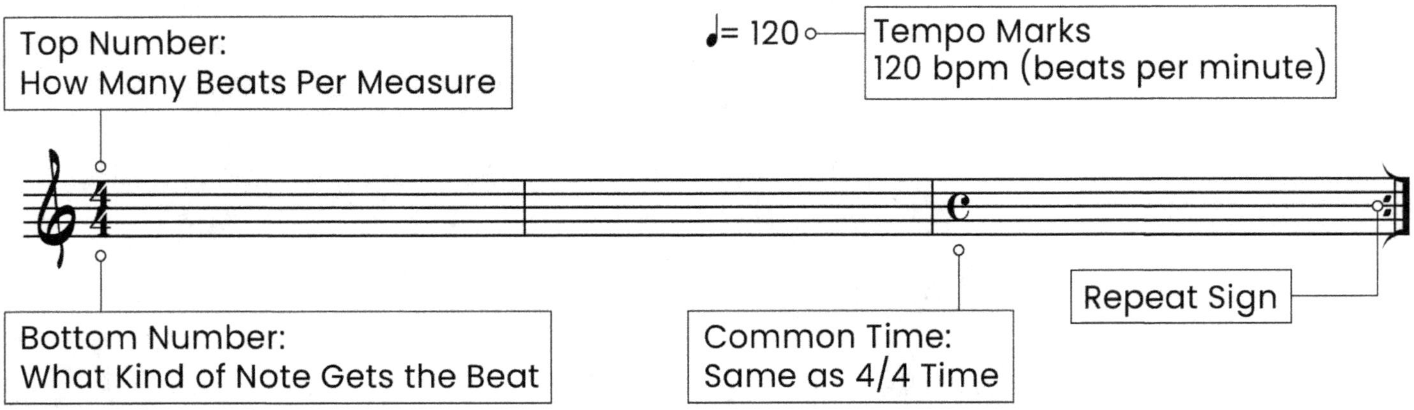

- Treble Clef or "G" Clef
- Staff
- Time Signature
- Measure Numbers
- Measure or Bar
- Bar Line
- End

- Top Number: How Many Beats Per Measure
- Bottom Number: What Kind of Note Gets the Beat
- Tempo Marks ♩= 120 bpm (beats per minute)
- Common Time: Same as 4/4 Time
- Repeat Sign

Notes On The Staff: There are seven notes in music (A, B, C, D, E, F, G) and they move up and down alphabetically on the staff.

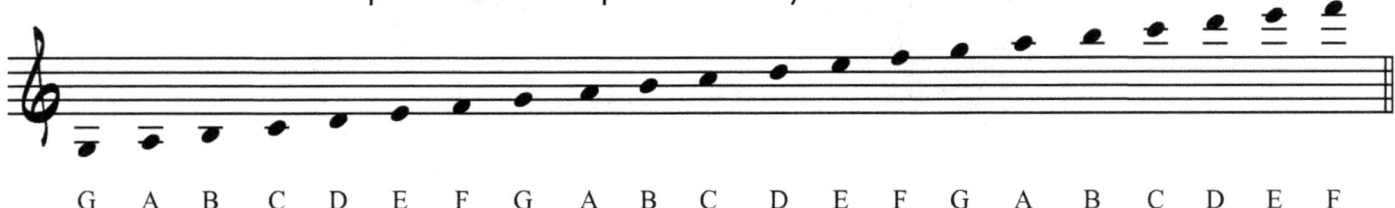

G A B C D E F G A B C D E F G A B C D E F

How To Remember The Notes:

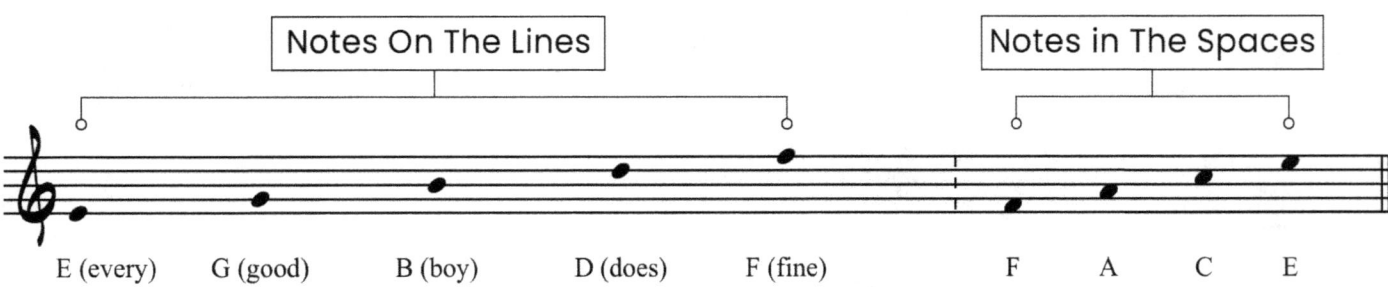

Notes On The Lines: E (every) G (good) B (boy) D (does) F (fine)

Notes in The Spaces: F A C E

A

HOW TO READ TAB

Tablature (TAB) is a form of music reading for guitarlele that uses a 6 line staff and numbers. Each line of the staff represents a string on the guitarlele and the numbers represent which fret you play on. When looking at the TAB staff it reads like it's upside down on the paper compared to the strings of your guitarlele. On the TAB staff, the highest line represents the 1st string (A string) of the guitarlele, while the lowest line represents the 6th string (A string) of the guitarlele. When you see 2 or more notes stacked on top of each other on the TABB staff, that means you play those notes at the same time, like a a chord.

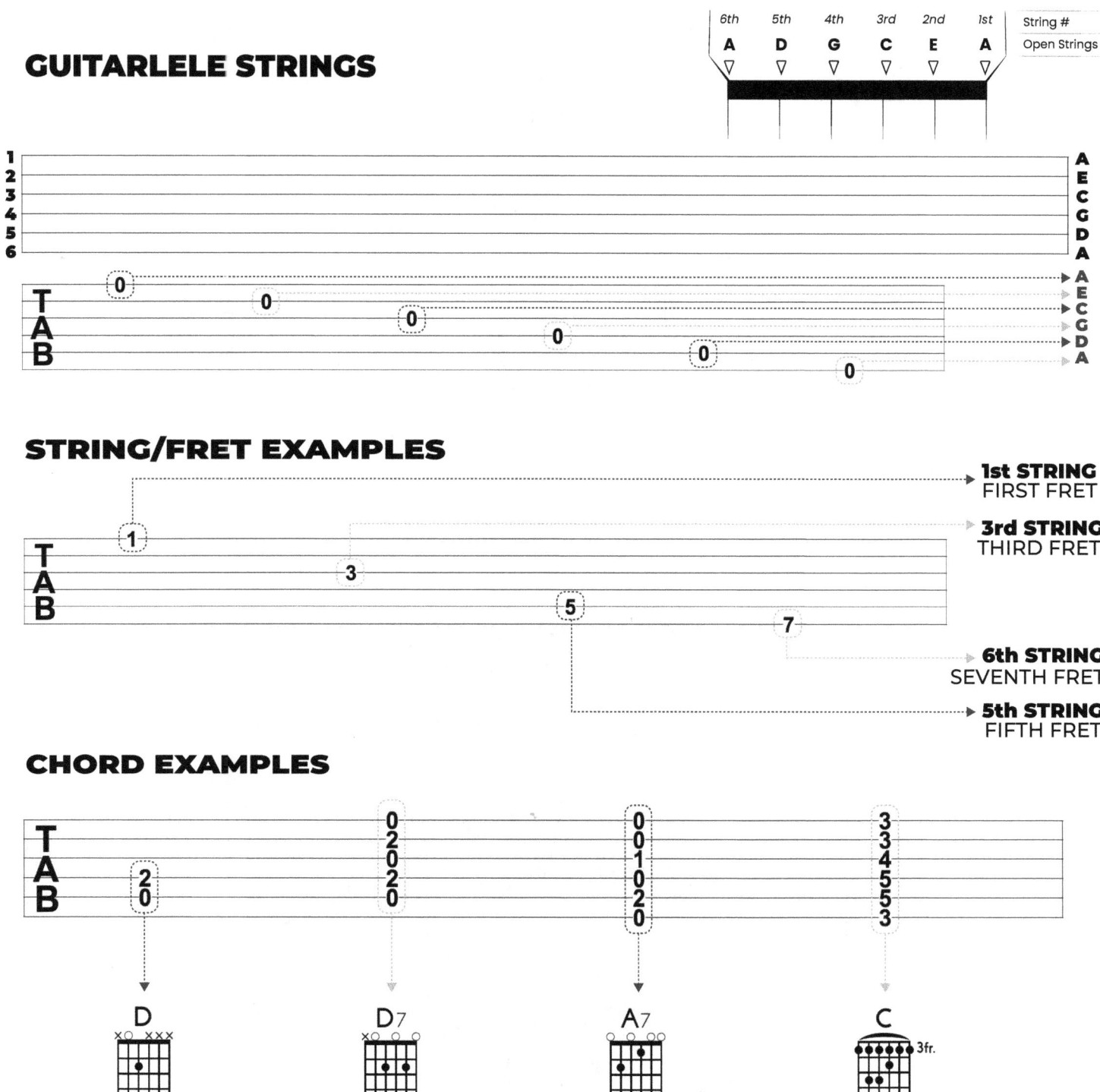

GUITARLELE PARTS

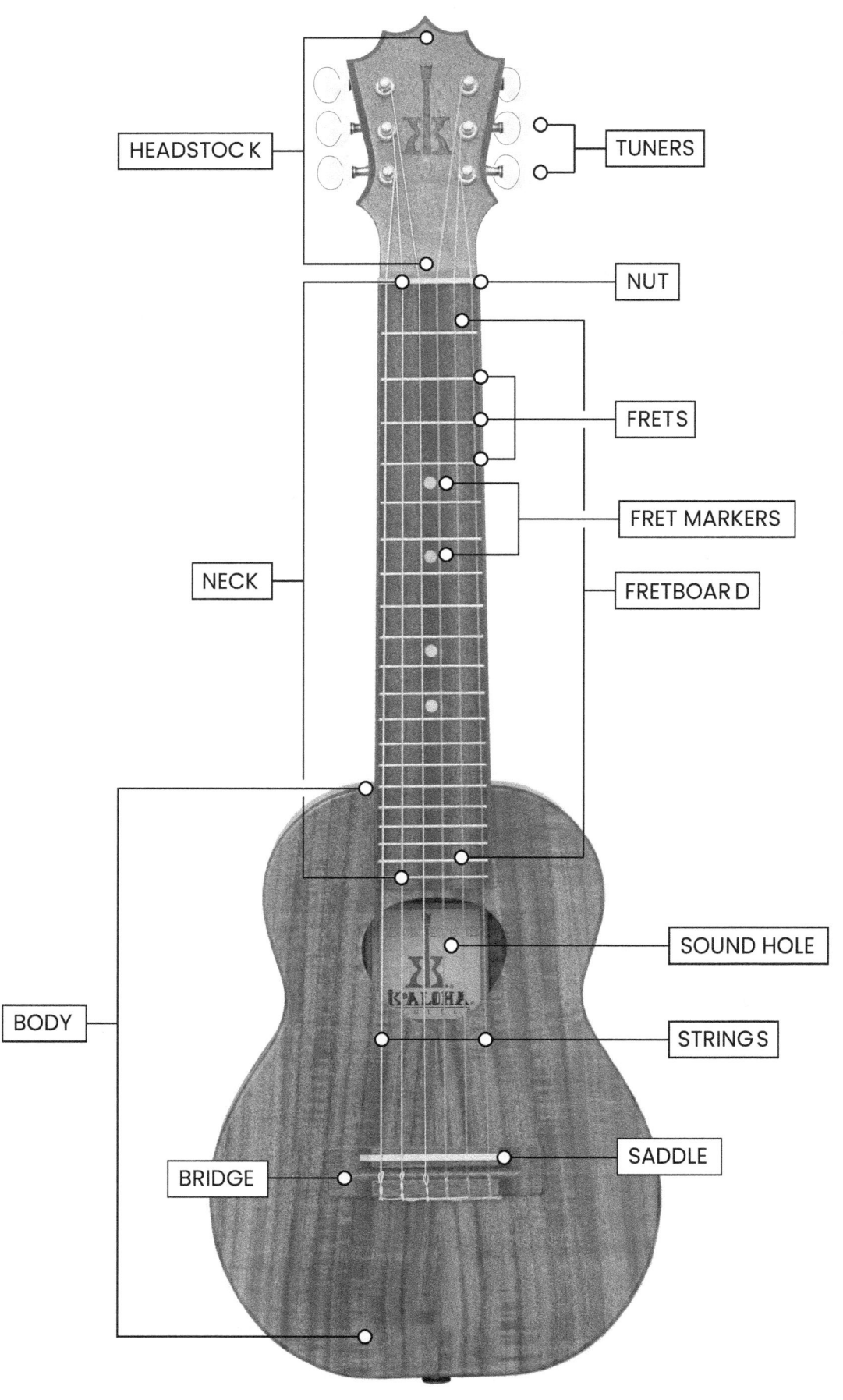

GUITARLELE HANDS

When playing fingerstyle on your guitarlele, you will see both letters and numbers to indicate which fingers to use both for picking hand and your fretting hand. These letters and numbers will show up in the music notation, TAB, and/or chord diagrams.

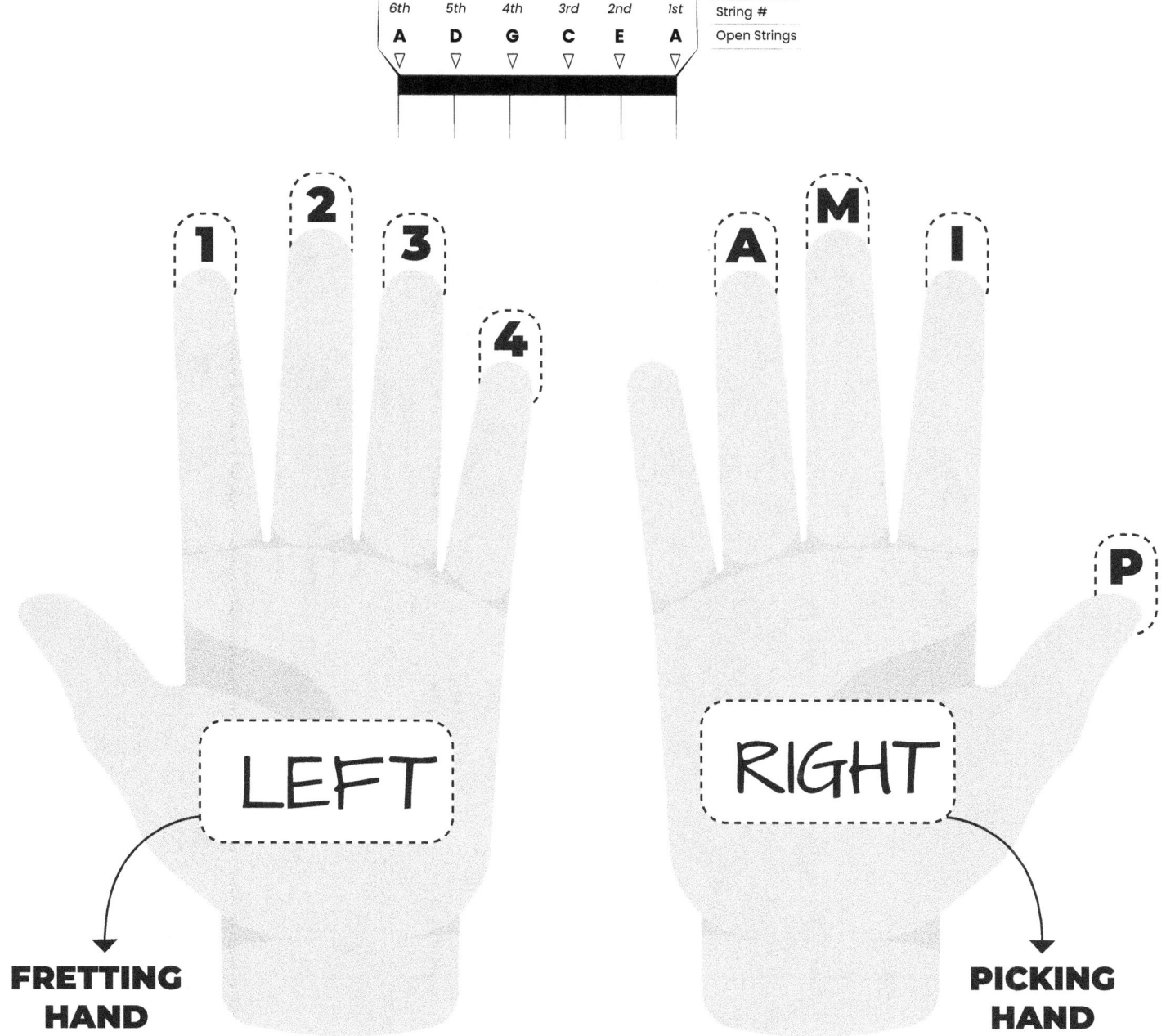

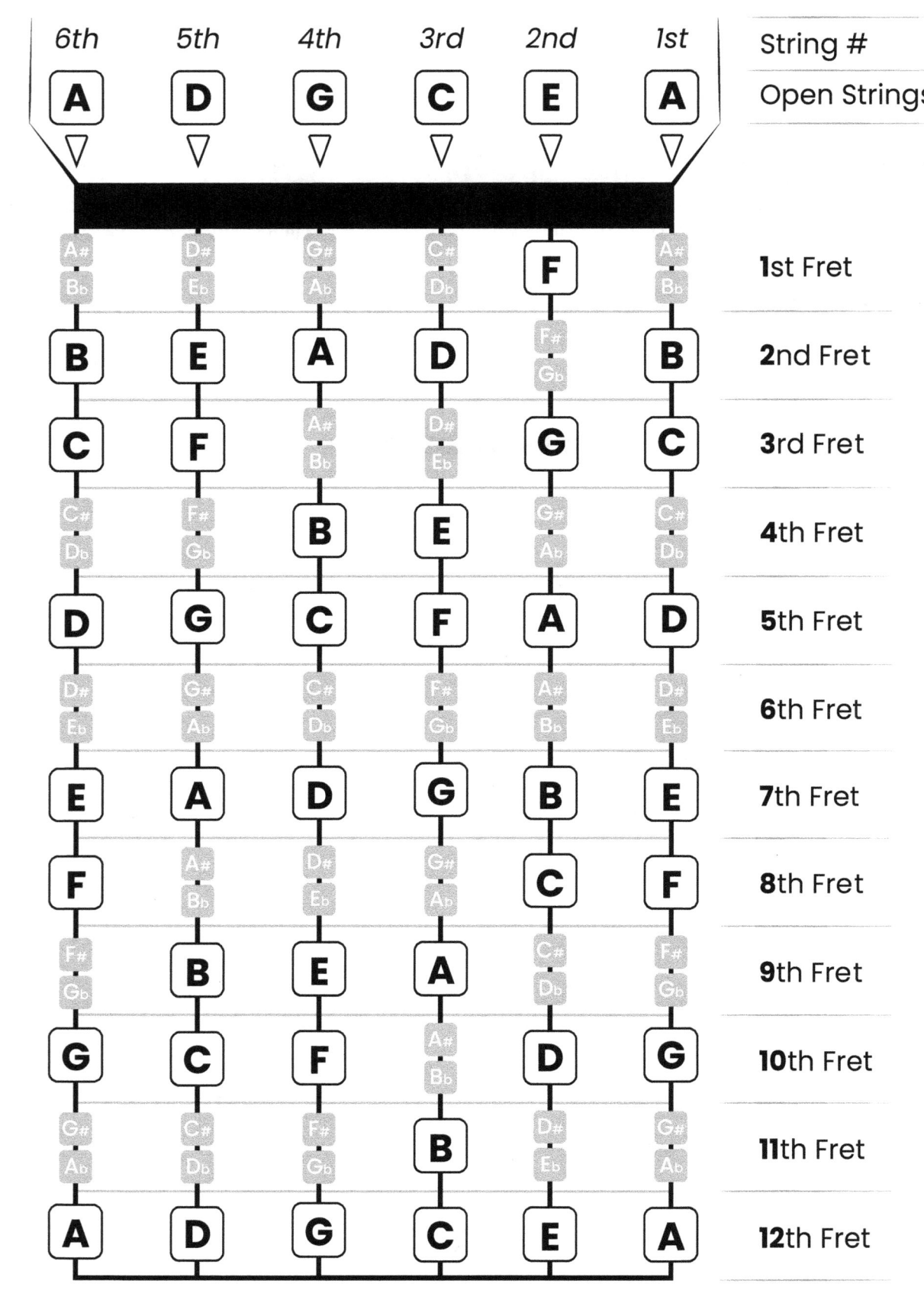

UNDERSTANDING CHORD DIAGRAMS

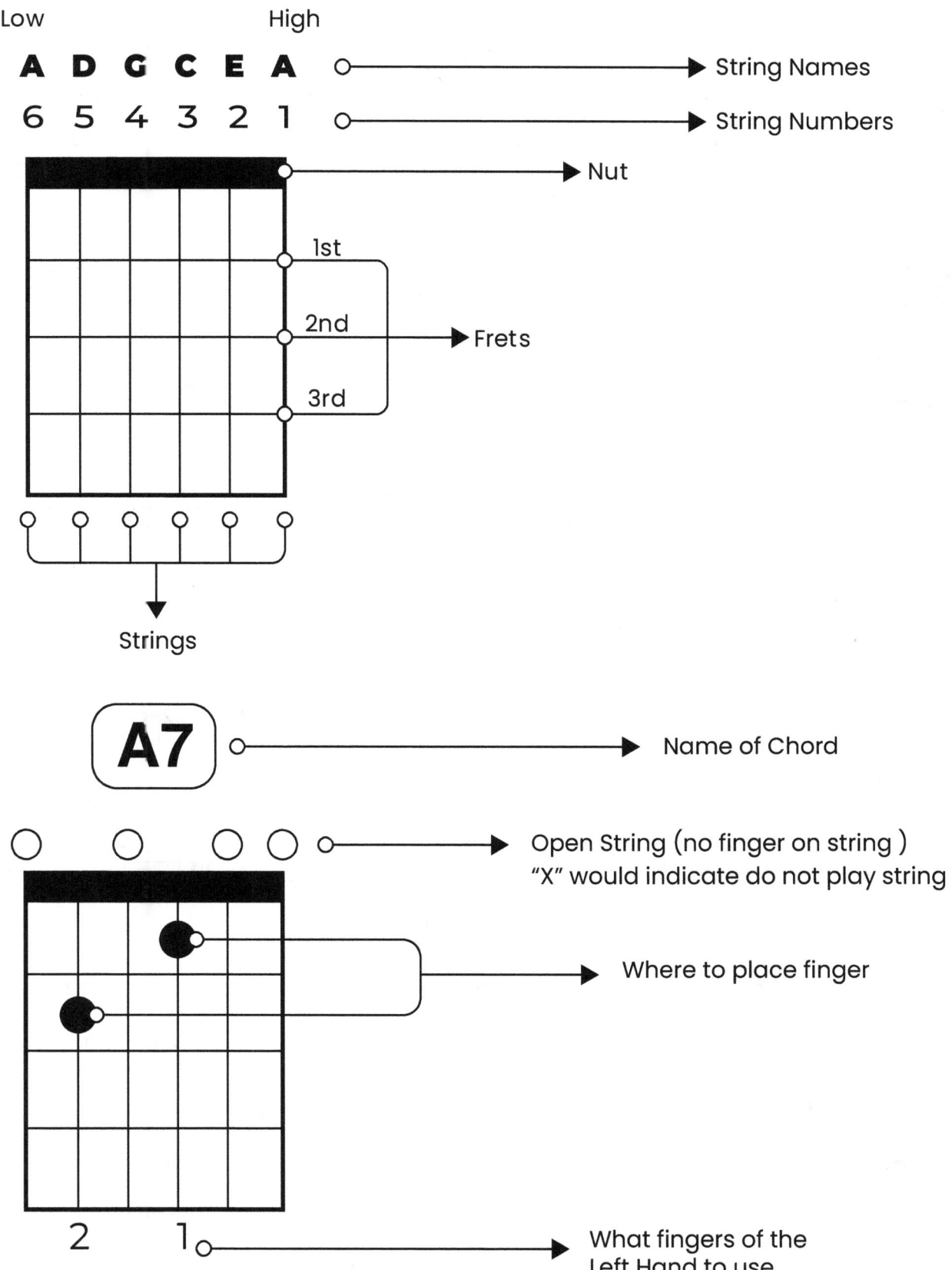

MUSIC SYMBOLS TO KNOW

A variety of symbols, articulations, repeats, hammer on's, pull off's, bends, and slides.

Fermata: Hold note

Staccato: Play note short

Accent: Play note loud

Accented Staccato: Play note loud + short

Vibrato: Rapid "shaking" of note

Arpeggiated Chord: Play the notes in fast succession from low to high strings

Grace Note: Fast embellishment note played before the main note

Mute: "Muffle" sound of strings either with left or right hand

Down Stroke: Pick string(s) with a downward motion

Up Stroke: Pick string(s) with an upward motion

Tie: Play first note but do not play second note that it is tied to

Ledger Lines: Extend the staff higher or lower.

Slash Notation: Repeat notes & rhythms from previous measure

1 Bar Repeat: Repeat notes & rhythms from previous measure

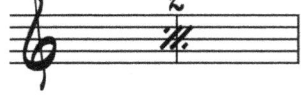
2 Bar Repeat: Repeat notes & rhythms from previous 2 measures

Repeat Sign: (Beginning)

Repeat Sign: (End)

1st Ending: Play this part the first time only

2nd Ending: Play this part the second time

(D.C. AL FINE) — *D.C.* (da capo) means go to the beginning of the tune and stop when you get to *Fine*

(D.C. AL CODA) — *D.C.* means go to the beginning of the tune and jump to *Coda* ⊕ when you see the sign ⊕

(D.S. AL FINE) — *D.S.* (dal segno) means go to the *Sign* 𝄋 and stop when you get to *Fine*

(D.S. AL CODA) — *D.S.* means go to the *Sign* 𝄋 And Jump to the *Coda* ⊕ when you see ⊕

SIM... — Play the same rhythm, strum pattern, or picking pattern as the previous measure

ETC... — Continue the same rhythm, strum pattern, or picking pattern as the previous measure

Hammer On:
Pick first note then hammer on to the next note without picking it.

Pull Off:
Pick first note then pull off to the next note without picking it.

Hammer On & Pull Off:
Pick first note, hammer on to the next note, and pull off to the last note all in one motion.

1/2 Step Bend:
Bend the first note a 1/2 step or 1 fret.

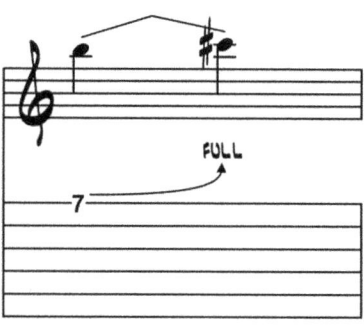

Whole Step Bend:
Bend the first note a whole step or 2 frets.

Step & 1/2 Bend:
Bend the first note 1 1/2 steps or 3 frets

Forward Slide:
Pick first note and slide up to higher note.

Backward Slide:
Pick first note and slide back to lower note.

Forward/Backward Slide:
Pick first note, slide up to next note and then slide back.

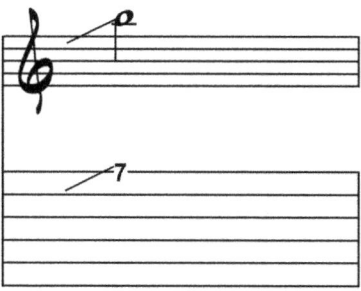

Slide Into Note:
Slide from 2-3 frets below note

Slide Off Note:
Slide off 2-5 frets after note

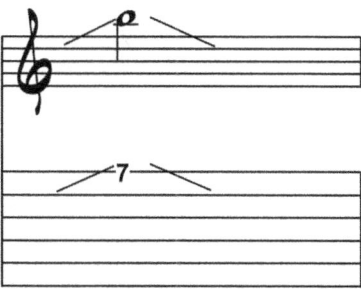

Slide Into Note then Slide Off Note

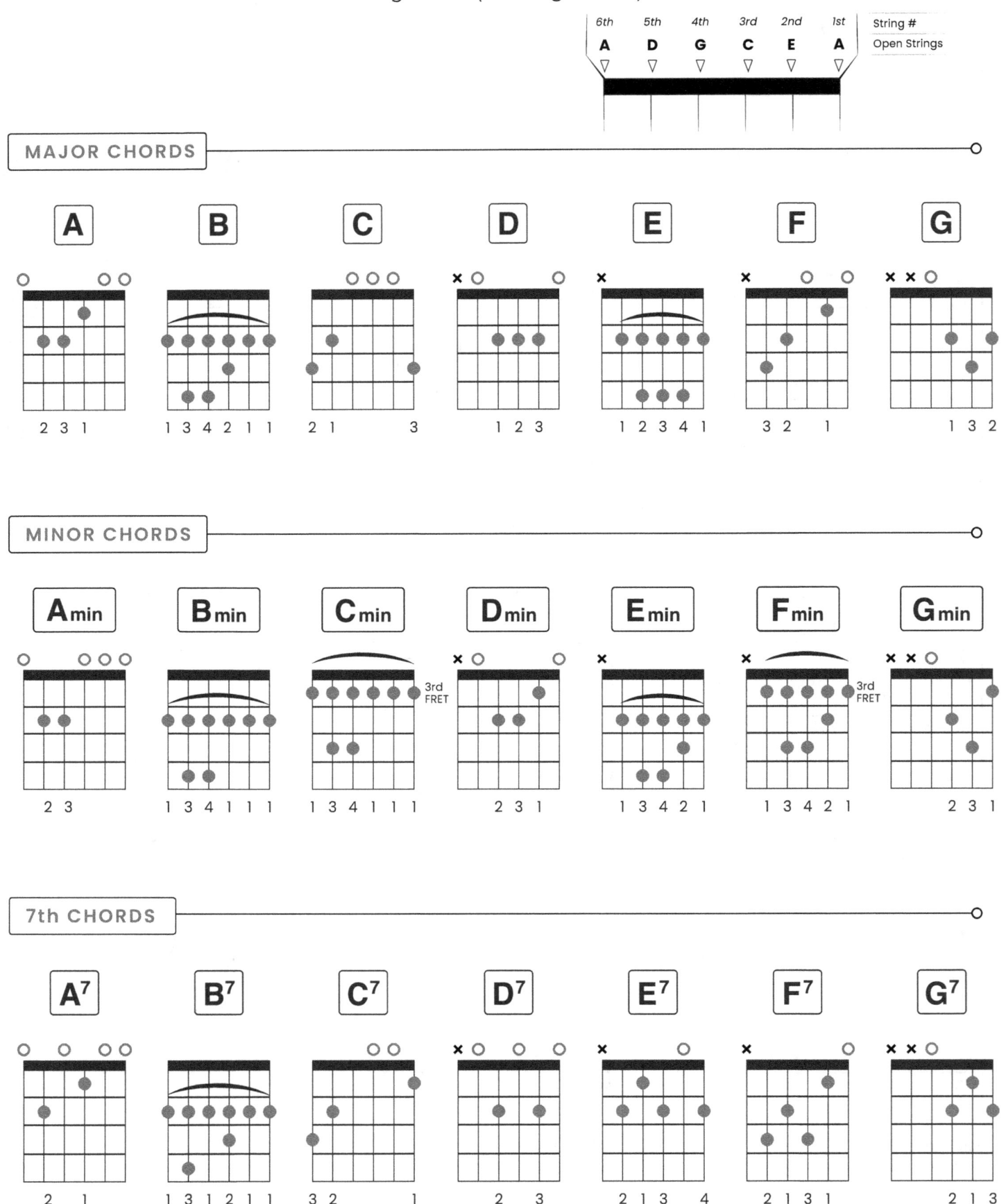

MAJOR 7th CHORDS

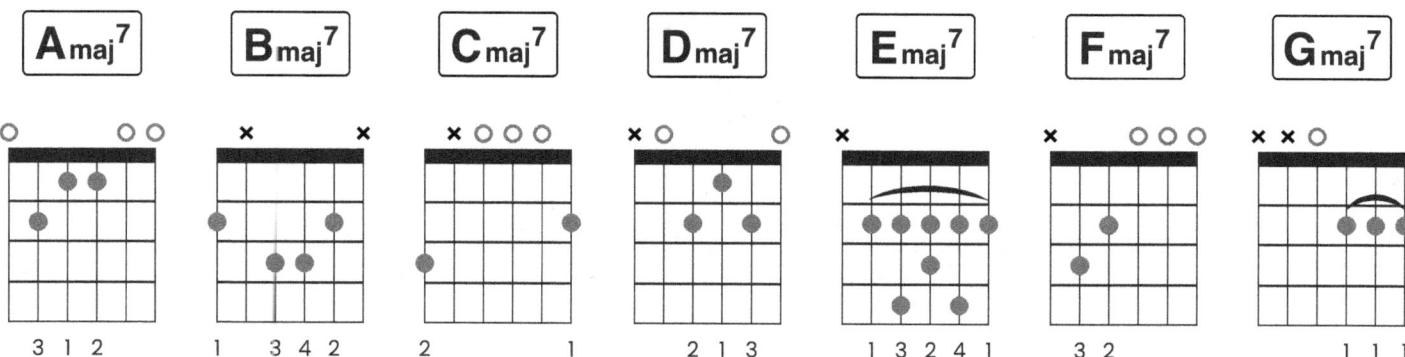

MINOR 7th CHORDS

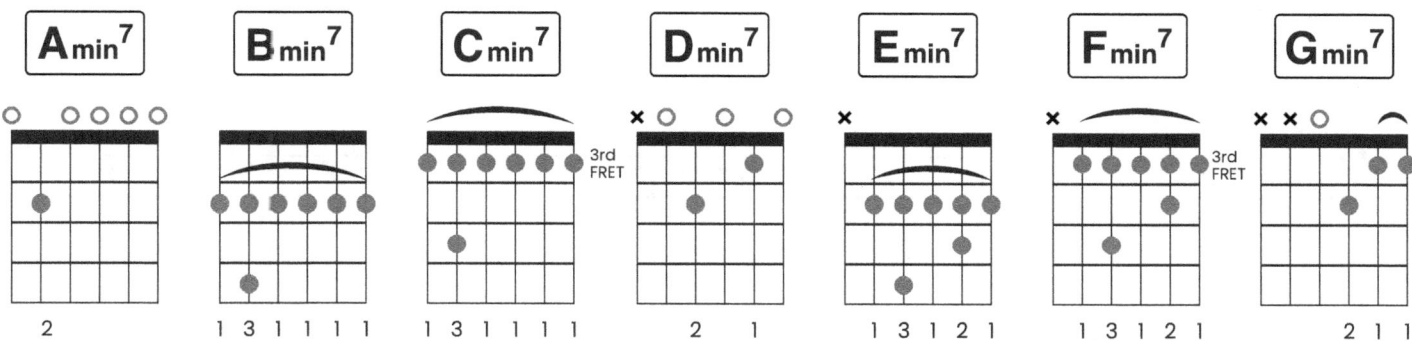

SUS + ADD CHORDS

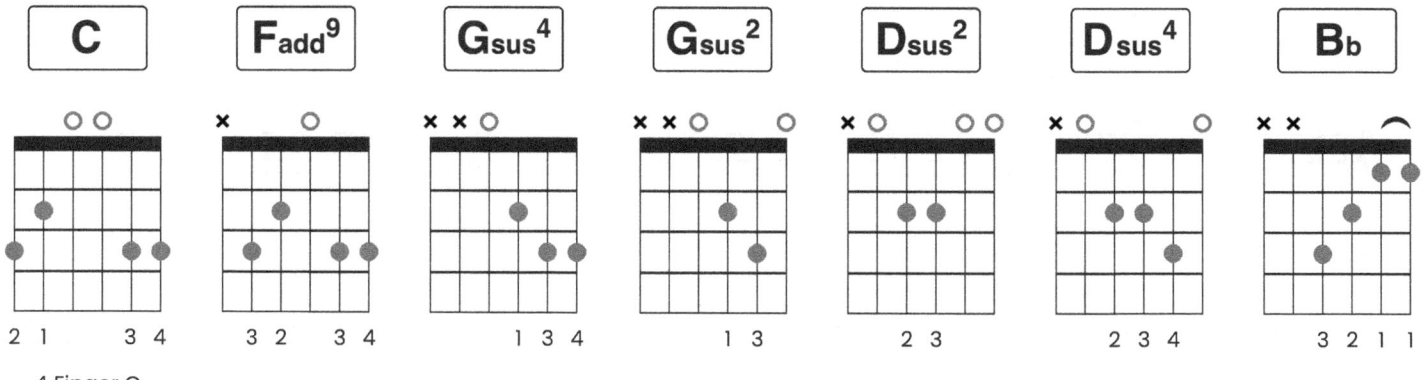

BASIC RHYTHMS

The 3 main rhythms in this lesson are whole notes, half notes and quarter notes.

ESSENTIAL RHYTHMS

The 4 main rhythms in this lesson are whole notes, half notes, quarter notes and eighth notes.

ABOUT THE AUTHOR

Terry Carter is a San Diego-based ukulele player, surfer, songwriter, and creator of ukelikethepros.com, rocklikethepros.com and terrycartermusicstore.com.
With over 25 years as a professional musician, educator and Los Angeles studio musician, Terry has worked with greats like Weezer, Josh Groban, Robby Krieger (The Doors), 2-time Grammy winning composer Christopher Tin (Calling All Dawns), Duff McKagan (Guns N' Roses), Grammy winning producer Charles Goodan (Santana/Rolling Stones), and the Los Angeles Philharmonic.
Terry has written and produced tracks for commercials (Discount Tire and Puma) and TV shows, including Scorpion (CBS), Pit Bulls & Parolees (Animal Planet), Trippin', Wildboyz, and The Real World (MTV). He has self-published over 25 books for Uke Like The Pros and Rock Like The Pros, filmed over 30 ukulele and guitar online courses, and has tens of millions of views on his docial media channels.
Terry received a Master of Music in Studio/Jazz Guitar Performance from University of Southern California and a Bachelor of Music from San Diego State University, with an emphasis in Jazz Studies and Music Education. He has taught at the University of Southern California, San Diego State University, Santa Monica College, Miracosta College, and Los Angeles Trade Tech College.

ONLINE UKULELE COURSES

The perfect place to learn how to play Ukulele, Baritone Ukulele, Guitar and Guitarlele.

ULTP Roadmap
WHERE TO START?

1) UKULELE BEGINNER
- A. Beginning Ukulele Starter Course
- B. Beginning Ukulele Bootcamp Course
- C. Ukulele Fundamentals Course
- D. Ukulele Practice & Technique Course
- E. Master the Ukulele 1

2) UKULELE INTERMEDIATE
- A. Master The Ukulele 2
- B. Beginning Music Reading
- C. 23 Ultimate Chord Progressions
- D. Beginning Ukulele Fingerstyle Course

3) UKULELE ADVANCED
- A. Ukulele Blues Mastery Course
- B. Beginning Ukulele Soloing Course
- C. Fingerstyle Mastery Course
- D. Jazz Swing Mastery Course

MORE OPTIONS!

FUNLAND
- A. Beginning Ukulele Kids Course Songbook
- B. 21 Popular Songs for Ukulele
- C. The Best Ukulele Christmas Songs
- D. 10 Classic Rock Licks
- E. Guitar Fundamentals

BARITONE UKULELE
- A. Beginning Baritone Ukulele Bootcamp Course
- B. 6 Weeks Baritone Q&A
- C. Baritone Blues Mastery Course
- D. Beginning Baritone Fingerstyle Course

GUITARLELE
- A. Guitarlele Starter Course
- B. 6 Weeks Guitarlele Q&A
- C. Guitarlele Course for Ukulele and Guitar Players
- D. Guitarlele Blues Mastery Course

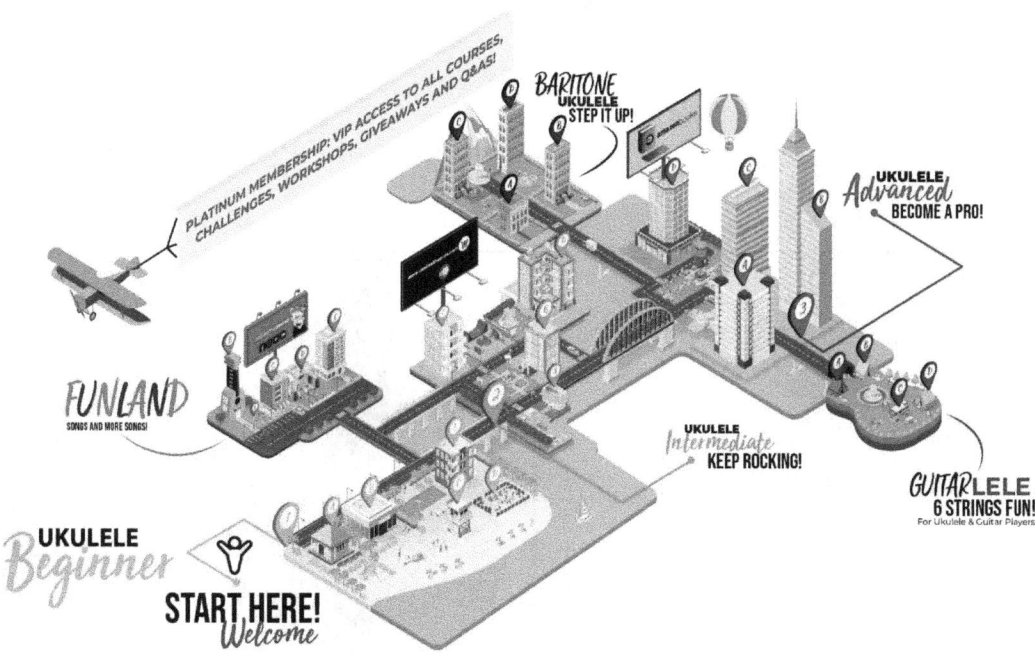

Courses For All Levels
UKELIKETHEPROS.COM

TERRY CARTER MUSIC STORE
All your music needs at the #1 music store, **terrycartermusicstore.com**

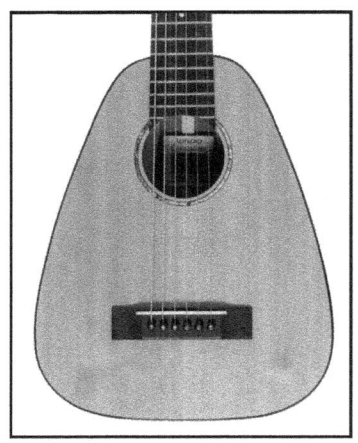
Guitarleles

Ukuleles

Guitars

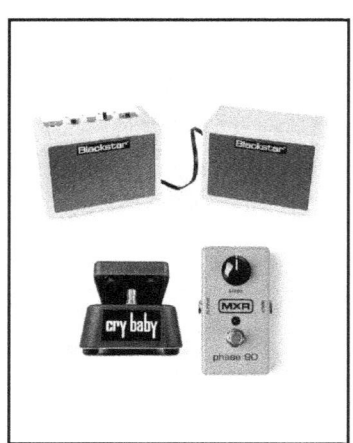
Amplifiers and Pedals

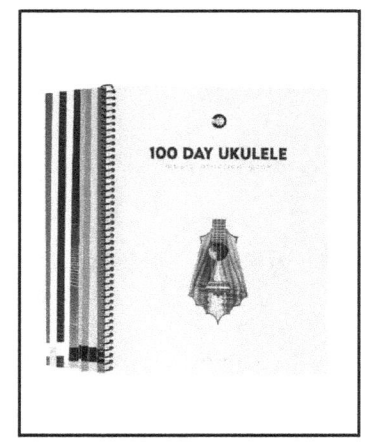
Books

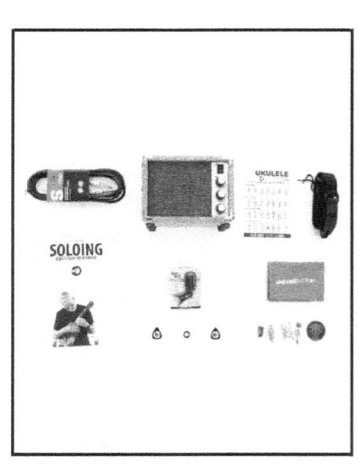
Accessories

UKELIKETHEPROS.COM
BLOG.UKELIKETHEPROS.COM
TERRYCARTERMUSICSTORE.COM
BUYSTRINGSONLINE.COM

@ukelikethepros

INTERESTED IN **GUITAR CONTENT?**
ROCKLIKETHEPROS.COM

www.ingramcontent.com/pod-product-compliance
Lightning Source LLC
Chambersburg PA
CBHW081356040426
42451CB00017B/3473